D1398525

To TREY,
Best Wishe

Bob Brodhead

SACKED!

Merry Christmas baby! — Love you. John

12-87

SACKED!

The Dark Side of Sports at Louisiana State University

BOB BRODHEAD
Former LSU Athletic Director

With MINDY BRODHEAD

Beauregard Press
Baton Rouge, Louisiana

Copyright © 1987
Robert E. Brodhead

All rights reserved. No part of this book may be reproduced or used in any form or by any means — graphic, electronic, or mechanical, including photocopying, recording, taping, filming, or information storage or retrieval systems — without written permission of the publisher.

Manufactured in the United States of America

Composition by Franklin Press, Inc.

Printer and binder: Arcata Graphics/Kingsport

Published and for sale by:

Beauregard Press
603 Europe Street
Baton Rouge, Louisiana 70802

Library of Congress Cataloging-in-Publication Data

Brodhead, Bob, 1937
   Sacked!

   1. Louisiana State University Agricultural and
Mechanical College--Athletics. 2. College sports--
Louisiana--Organization and administration--Case
studies. 3. Brodhead, Bob, 1937-   . 4. Coaches
(Athletics)--United States--Biography. I. Brodhead,
Mindy, 1960-   . II. Title.
GV691.L68B76   1987   796'.092'4 (B)   87-31822
ISBN 0-944679-00-5

Library of Congress Catalog Card Number
87-073036

ISBN 0-944679-00-5

For the love of my life, Kay, a feisty lady small of stature but a mountain of support. She loved LSU as I did, with all her heart.

For my children, Mindy, Amy and Jason, whose love reassured me and whose strength made me proud.

Special Acknowledgment

This book in its final stages turned out just the way I had hoped due to the efforts of my editor, Mindy Brodhead. She labored long and hard transcribing our story. Her familiarity with the story line was firsthand; then she added a special ingredient — love.

"Through many dangers, toils, and snares,
    "I have already come.
" 'Tis grace hath brought me safe
    "thus far,
"And grace will lead me home."

Amazing Grace

John Newton

Acknowledgments

To the people who worked in my inner sanctum, I thank you for your loyalties, championships and profits, a winning formula.

Members of my staff: Ed Atlas, Pat Dale, Donald Ray Kennard, Paul Lindgren, Mike Mallet, Jon McBride, Bill McClure, Pat O'Toole, Virginia Robertson, Jim Sullivan, James Thomas, Arthur Triche, Scott Woodburn and Joe Yates.

My coaches: Buddy Alexander, Karen Bahnsen, Skip Bertman, Phillip Campbell, Sam Freas, Sue Gunter, Scott Luster, Billy Maxwell, "D-D" Pollock, Loren Seagrave and Jerry Simmons.

I'd also like to thank Norman and Beth Ferachi of Beauregard Press for their invaluable assistance.

CARROLL SECURITY CONSULTANTS, INC.

4560 North Blvd., Suite 115
Baton Rouge, LA 70806
(504)927-6907

3101 W. Napoleon, Suite 225
Metairie, LA 70001
(504) 831-0911

1304 Bertrand, Suite A-2
Lafayette, LA 70506
(318) 237-6384

October 2, 1987

TO WHOM IT MAY CONCERN:

On October 2, 1987, Mr. Robert E. Brodhead voluntarily came to this polygraph suite for a polygraph examination.

The main issue under consideration was whether or not Mr. Brodhead was telling the truth when he claimed that the information contained in his book "Sacked" is true and correct to the best of his knowledge.

The facts concerning this case were provided the polygraphist by Mr. Brodhead.

Before his pre-test interview, Mr. Brodhead voluntarily signed a permission form stating that he was taking the examination of his own free will. A photo-copy of this executed form is enclosed with this report; the original has been incorporated as a part of our case files.

In the polygraph recordings, there were definite indications of truthfulness when Mr. Brodhead answered "NO" to the following pertinent test questions:

> "Are you lying, when you say that, to the best of your knowledge, all the facts in your book "Sacked" are true and correct?"

> "Regarding your book "Sacked", did you purposely include material that, to the best of your knowledge was not truthful?"

> "To the best of your knowledge, did you purposely include information in your book "Sacked" that was not truthful and correct?"

It is the opinion of the polygraphist, based upon the polygraph examination of Mr. Brodhead, that he is telling the truth to the above pertinent test questions.

Respectfully submitted,
CARROLL SECURITY CONSULTANTS, INC.

Larry Carroll

Larry Carroll
Certified Polygraphist

Enclosure

LC/fb

Larry Carroll is a 1970 graduate of the National Training Center of Polygraph Science, New York, New York. He is a former lieutenant with the East Baton Rouge Parish Sheriff's Office, where he was in charge of their polygraph section. Carroll has served as President, Secretary-Treasurer and Director of the Louisiana Polygraph Association. He served as a member of the Board of Directors and Vice President of the American Polygraph Association for seven years. Larry is the founder of and an instructor at the Carroll Institute of Polygraphy. The Carroll Institute is Louisiana's only polygraph school approved by the Louisiana Department of Education and the American Polygraph Association. He is Certified by the State of Louisiana and fully licensed in Mississippi and Texas to practice polygraphy. Larry Carroll is President of Carroll Security Industries with offices in Baton Rouge, Lafayette and New Orleans.

Joseph A. Oster and Company, Inc.

704 MILL STREET • WEST MONROE, LOUISIANA 71291 • (318) 388-0411

October 6, 1987

TO WHOM IT MAY CONCERN:

Re: Polygraph Examination of Robert E. Brodhead

The undersigned is presently Chairman of the State of Louisiana Polygraph Board and a Private Investigator and Polygraphist.

On October 6, 1986, at the request of Mr. Larry Carroll, the Writer conducted a comprehensive review and analysis of the polygraph examination of Mr. Robert E. Brodhead.

My analysis consisted of a review of the questions formulated and asked during the examination, the polygrams created, and the overall format and technique utilized.

The zone of comparison control question technique utilized by the polygraphist was validated in a study conducted for the U.S. Department of Justice at the University of Utah under contract number 75-N1-99-0001. The technique appears to have sufficient strength of issue, distinctness of issue and case information available for the examiner to have expected a conclusive determination.

The polygraphist, Larry Carroll, has seventeen years of polygraph experience, graduated from a polygraph school accredited by the American Polygraph Association, and is the holder of general polygraph licenses issued by Louisiana, Mississippi and Texas.

The polygraphist has properly applied the zone of comparison technique in that question spacing, intra-chart adjustments and markings all appear to be within the prescribed tolerances. I performed a numerical analysis on the polygrams utilizing the scoring system validated under the aforementioned study. In this system, a +6 or above indicates a lack of deception, or truthfulness, in the examinee's answers to the relevant questions. A -6 or below indicates deception or untruthfulness in the examinee's answers to the relevant questions. A -5 to +5 is "inconclusive". To score an examinee "deceptive" when the person is in fact "truthful" would require the scoring to be "off" 12 points.

My analysis of the three scoreable polygrams resulted in an overall score of +14 indicating that Robert E. Brodhead was truthful when he answered all relevant questions "NO".

Reviewing Polygraphist:
JOSEPH A. OSTER AND COMPANY, INC.

Joseph A. Oster
JAO/fb

LEGAL • BUSINESS • INSURANCE INVESTIGATIONS • POLYGRAPHS • SECURITY CONSULTANTS

Table of Contents

Prologue

I'd often heard it said that committing one's thoughts to paper is therapeutic. When I found myself full of hurt and confusion over the untimely demise of my career as Athletic Director of Louisiana State University, I picked up a pen and hoped that what I'd heard was true.

I began by writing sketchy notes of the people and events that played a role in my decision to resign on October 21, 1986. Soon, I was marvelling at the way the elements, like pieces of a jigsaw puzzle, were emerging and fitting together. One night, after a particularly long session spent scribbling my thoughts as quickly as my hand would write them, I said to Kay, my wife, "You know, this stuff is unbelievable. It's like a who-dun-it mystery."

She nodded. "I know. Sometimes it doesn't seem possible that we actually lived through it."

Then she looked at me and said, "Why don't you write a book?"

And so I have.

This is my story, the story of four-and-a-half years spent on a roller coaster ride of exhilarating highs and gut-wrenching lows. It's the story, as they say, of the good, the bad and the ugly . . .

Of the tens of thousands of loyal, loving fans who make Tiger Stadium the most feared field of competition in college athletics.

Of the middle-aged men who wear their bright purple pants and gold tee shirts to football games, and their middle-aged wives who don't mind.

Of Death Valley and the Deaf Dome.

Of All-Sports trophies and Final Fours, College World Series and Sugar Bowls.

Of disloyalty and deceit.

Of FBI stings and Ethics Commission investigations.

Of friends and enemies.

I want to believe that the forces that worked to undermine me and my administration do not exist at other colleges and universities.

I want to believe that nowhere else is an athletic director as visible as the state's governor; that nowhere else would a lieutenant governor threaten to introduce to the state's legislature a resolution to fire the athletic director over two Final Four basketball tickets.

I want to believe that everywhere else, the athletic program is athletes and coaches, fun and games, not a dangerous trap where people get hurt and careers get ruined.

But you'll have to be the judge of that.

As I wrote my story, I couldn't help but see the many similarities between my career as an athletic director and the many years I spent playing quarterback.

As a quarterback, I often encountered seemingly impossible situations: fourth and long, time running out, behind on the scoreboard. Those were the kinds of challenges I lived for.

So was the job as LSU's Athletic Director. When I accepted the position in May of 1982, the Athletic Department was more than a million dollars in the red. The football team had just posted its worst record in the past quarter-century. And the overall athletic program had tied for eighth place in the ten-member Southeastern Conference.

Four-and-a-half years later, there were $9 million in profits on the books and back-to-back Bernie Moore trophies, significant of the best overall men's athletic program in the conference, in the trophy case.

But I was gone.

As a quarterback, I had always been lucky. No matter how many times during a game I'd get sacked, I was always able to pick myself up and return to the action.

As the Athletic Director of LSU, I wasn't so fortunate.

CHAPTER ONE

The Road to LSU

Along a western Pennsylvania stretch of the Allegheny River, there are dozens of small, rural communities inhabited by a rugged cross section of farmers, miners and steel workers. These are sturdy, hardworking people, rich in ethnic heritage and pride. Nowhere is this pride more evident, however, than in the love the people of western Pennsylvania have for their local high school sports teams.

Kittanning, Pa., a sleepy little town of 6,000, is just such a place. It is also my hometown.

In Kittanning, heroes were measured by the number of varsity letters worn on a red and white letterman's jacket. Mine boasted nine, so from the beginning of my athletic career, I enjoyed a great deal of visibility.

I played football, basketball and baseball for the Wildcats of Kittanning High, but it was my quarterbacking abilities for which I was most widely known.

There was an abundance of talented young football players residing throughout western Pennsylvania, and college recruiters were kept busy visiting the many area high school football stadiums each autumn Friday night. At the end of my senior year in 1954, I was offered athletic scholarships to Pitt, Penn State, Michigan State, Ohio State, SMU, Maryland, West Virginia, Clemson, South Carolina, North Carolina and Duke, among others. I'm not sure there was ever any question as to where I'd end up.

The sports editor of Kittanning's one and only newspaper was a graduate of Duke University, and his constant attention, as well as his sometimes overly complimentary game write-ups, had me headed for Durham, N.C., before I knew what hit me.

In retrospect, Duke University was perhaps the best choice I could have made in a college. A diploma from this highly respected institution, and the dedication it would take to earn it, would prove invaluable to my business career. At the time, however, all I cared about when I hit the Duke campus was becoming a part of the great Blue Devil football tradition.

Much to my surprise, life as a college freshman entailed more than football practice and game days. I also found myself facing academic challenges the likes of which I had never imagined. Remember, the vast majority of my high school life was spent earning my nine varsity letters.

At Duke, Dr. Martin Black, the head of the accounting department, was assigned to be my faculty advisor. Dr. Black decided that I was going to major in accounting if it killed him. And it nearly did.

Debits by the blackboard, credits by the window . . .

Debits by the blackboard, credits by the window . . .

Easy enough. Imagine my surprise, then, when at the end of the first semester, I was within a gnat's hair of failing out of school for a lack of the required quality points.

It was, ironically, a bout with appendicitis and the ensuing red-shirt period that saved my tail. Forced to sit on the sidelines for the 1955 season, I grew up a little bit, and my grade point average improved at about the same pace.

I returned to the football field to start twenty-six games at quarterback for the Blue Devils, although under the run-oriented game plans of Coach Bill Murray, I often thought of myself as the offense's third guard.

But I learned from Murray, a maker of men, and today, I credit him with instilling in me a desire to succeed and an unwillingness to quit, no matter what the obstacles. The man was a slave driver, pure and simple, but he challenged me to be a winner. That, along with my hard-earned accounting degree from one of the nation's most prestigious universities, gave me a firm foundation on which to build an athletic career which would span the next twenty-nine years of my life and include administrative positions in professional as well as college sports.

I was taken in the twelfth round of the 1958 college draft by the Cleveland Browns of the National Football League. I had a year of college eligibility remaining, however, and I returned to Duke for my senior season.

During the summer of 1958, I drove to Cleveland with my childhood sweetheart and wife-to-be, Kay Spicher, to look for a place to live, a teaching position for her and off-season employment for me. Never once did it enter my mind that a non-passing quarterback fresh out of college might have some difficulty fitting into the most sophisticated passing offense in the NFL, orchestrated by the ingenious Paul Brown. After all, Otto Graham had been a tailback at Northwestern until Brown turned him into an all-star quarterback.

While in Cleveland, I interviewed with several accounting firms, and Haskins & Sells, a national big-eight firm, offered me an off-season position as a junior accountant with the understanding that for five months of the year, I would be pursuing my dream of playing professional football.

The Browns offered me a $9,000 contract, no signing bonus, and the opportunity to add to my compensation the following season if I made the active roster. I didn't. Immediately after I graduated in January of 1959, I began my six-month military obligation, and when I couldn't secure an early release, I was forced to report to the Brown's training camp two weeks late. By the time I finally arrived, I found the other quarterback hopefuls with an insurmountable head start.

When Paul Brown released me, he asked that I report to the Saskatchewan Rough Riders of the Canadian Football League to get some game experience. I did just that, arriving in a foreign land to play a foreign game and wondering, all the while, if this was the life of a professional football player that I had dreamed about.

At the end of the 1959 season, I returned to Cleveland to begin my training with Haskins & Sells. Shortly after I arrived, I received a telephone call from the Buffalo Bills of the new American Football League. When they invited me to report to the next year's training camp, I knew I'd seen my last Canadian winter.

I made the Bills' roster. In fact, I started several games, but six weeks into the 1960 season, I was released. Once again, I packed my bags and headed for home.

Dreams die hard, however, and at age twenty-four, I wasn't ready to hang up the cleats. Cleveland had just landed a franchise in the new United Football League, and shortly before the start of the 1961 season, I signed a contract with the Cleveland Bulldogs. My salary? Fifty bucks a game.

The Bulldogs played their home games at the Cloverleaf Speedway, a converted stock car race track with about 5,000 seats, very few of which were ever filled when we played football there. Where the playing surface ended, the cement race track began, and bales of hay were placed around the field's edge in hopes of preventing serious injury to players running out of bounds. It's a miracle no one ever crashed through the hay and got run over by a stock car on a practice run.

The lights at Cloverleaf weren't quite high enough to be considered football lights. A long pass, arched skyward down the field, would literally disappear for several seconds, making for some truly acrobatic receptions on the other end.

We didn't have locker rooms, either. Post-game showers consisted of a garden hose and lots of soap. One year, we sent our player rep to complain to management about the lack of facilities, and he returned with a second hose.

Once, when we were headed for Toledo for a game against the Tornadoes, the transmission on our chartered bus fell out. We limped into a Howard Johnson's rest stop on the Ohio Turnpike and began placing emergency phone calls to the bus company. Unfortunately, the company hadn't been paid for the last trip, and they refused to send another bus to pick us up.

Word of our predicament reached the Toledo stadium, and someone made an announcement over the public address system that the Bulldogs were stranded about twenty miles out along the road. Forty or so fans volunteered to come out and get us.

While we waited, the trainer unloaded his gear and set up shop, taping our ankles on the rest stop's picnic tables. It was quite a sight.

It was dark when the caravan arrived, and our 8 p.m. kickoff time had come and gone. By the time we finally made it to the stadium, it was after 10 p.m., and the referees wouldn't let us warm up. It probably didn't matter. There wasn't anybody left to watch us play.

What made it even worse was that the governor of Ohio had been invited to the game by the Tornadoes' owners, who were anxious to prove that Toledo could support a pro team. He finally went home, too.

Needless to say, the conditions under which the Bulldogs played football were less than ideal. They certainly gave a whole new meaning to competing in the face of adversity.

At the conclusion of the 1963 season, I was once again invited to try out with the Cleveland Browns. My second attempt at making the team netted the same results as my first, however, and I returned to the Bulldogs for the 1964 season.

By that time, the team had moved to Canton, Ohio, some seventy miles to the south. Several other Cleveland-based players had signed contracts, and four nights a week, we'd make the long round-trip to take part in practice sessions.

Looking back, I don't know how — or why — we did it, but at the time, none of us seemed to mind. We were young, and we were playing the game we loved.

Our dedication was rewarded at the conclusion of the 1964 season when the Canton Bulldogs beat the Indianapolis Warriors in the UFL championship game. Ironically, just before kickoff, the league announced that the Canton vicinity was incapable of supporting a professional football team. We were the first homeless champions in the UFL's brief history.

During the summer of 1965, a group of backers was found in Philadelphia, Pa., to finance the team as a member of the newly formed Continental Football League. The Bulldogs were on the road again, but this time, it looked like they were going without their quarterback. I couldn't afford to quit my job in Cleveland and move to Philly for what I made playing football.

But the team's new owners wanted me as part of the package. I had been named the UFL's most valuable player in 1961, and again in 1964, and the Bulldogs' brass thought my signing with the team would help create fan interest and support. They offered to fly me in from Cleveland two nights a week to practice, and then to wherever the team played each weekend. I gladly accepted their flattering offer.

Mondays, Tuesdays and Wednesdays during the season saw me hard at work as general manager of A.J. Gates Company, a Cleveland-based material handling firm. Late Wednesday afternoons, I'd hop a plane for the fifty-minute flight to Philadelphia. I'd practice on Wednesday and Thursday evenings, sleeping at the Germantown YMCA, fly home for work on Fridays, then join the team on Saturdays in cities from Toronto, Canada, to Orlando, Fla. I never knew which was the more time-consuming chore, developing our offensive game plans, or arranging my flight schedules.

Following the 1965 season, the Bulldogs hired Wayne Hardin, former head coach at the Naval Academy, to be head coach and general manager. As coach, he was to win football games. As GM, he was to cut expenses at the same time.

The cost of my Cleveland-to-Philadelphia commutes must have stuck out like a sore thumb, and Hardin informed the Bulldogs' owners that he didn't like the arrangement. Back in Cleveland, I had yet to meet the man, and it was beginning to look as if I never would. He apparently didn't want a travelling quarterback.

The owners, however, insisted that I was to remain a part of the team, no matter what it took. I wanted $20,000 a year to make the move. Hardin refused, but the owners stood firm, and after some serious negotiations, a compromise was reached. As the 1966 season began, Hardin found himself with an assistant coach, assistant general manager, corporate treasurer, business manager and all-star quarterback. While I waited for my family to join me from Cleveland, Hardin also found himself with a roommate. He didn't like that any better than my exorbitant salary.

By the end of the season, however, Hardin had experienced a change of heart, especially after I'd thrown thirty-nine touchdown passes, plus another four during the play-offs, and led the team to the 1966 CFL championship with a 20-17 overtime victory over the Orlando Panthers.

The many hats I wore during the 1966 season taught me a great deal about the art of sports management. Game days were particularly educational.

Up early and at Temple Stadium before 9 a.m., I'd check out each ticket window, make sure the programs had been delivered and pass along attendance estimates to the concessionaire. Shortly after noon, I'd return home for lunch and a few hours' rest before heading back to the stadium by 4 p.m. for another round of the ticket windows. By the time my teammates began filtering in at 5:30, I'd already put in a full day's work.

During warm-up, I'd estimate a house count and figure a projected per capita in concessions sales. By kickoff, I'd know if there would be sufficient cash flow to cover player payroll. If there wasn't, I never told the team about it until after the game. I didn't like the prospect of my offensive line finding out at halftime that we had a case of "the shorts."

Shortly after the conclusion of the Bulldogs' championship season, the *National Observer* ran a story about the unique combination of jobs I performed for the team. Art Modell, the innovative young owner of the Cleveland Browns, read the piece and decided I might make a good addition to his management team. Either that, or he was afraid I'd come back to Cleveland and try out for the Browns for the third time.

Modell offered me the job of business manager, and when I couldn't find anyone to talk me out of taking it, I called it quits on my football career and moved my family back to Cleveland.

We were building a house just outside Philadelphia, and it upset Kay to sell it before we had a chance to live in it. By that time, however, she was beginning to get the picture. Football wives don't grow roots.

Armed with firsthand experience in deficit financing and the ability to get the most out of a dollar, I reported to the Browns' office complex in Municipal Stadium in the spring of 1967. Modell enthusiastically welcomed me aboard, but it was apparent that the new kid on the block, who hit the door talking about budgets, posed something of a threat to those who filled the many patronage positions within the Browns' organization. To date, the club had operated under few, if any, financial restrictions, and my arrival signalled the beginning of a new management philosophy.

I spent my first several years with the Browns learning everything I could about the inner workings of a professional football franchise.

Jim Sullivan, the Browns' ticket manager, taught me as much as I could absorb about the ticket business, and what Sullivan doesn't know isn't worth learning. Having served as ticket manager of the Philadelphia Phillies for seventeen years prior to joining the Browns, Sullivan was the best possible mentor, and he taught me everything from working the window to why ticket people are the most cantankerous of all sports personnel.

I learned about marketing and promotions from John Minco, the Browns' promotions manager. Minco could have been a general manager on most NFL clubs on the strength of his street savvy, not to mention his knowledge of the media. In the days when sports marketing was unheard of, Minco was inventing lucky-number programs and crowd-building gimmicks.

I was assigned administrative oversight of the Browns' concessions, a duty I gladly assumed. Concessions had been a favorite of mine since my days of counting hot dogs and soft drinks with the Bulldogs, and I was anxious to see how the big boys handled this potentially lucrative operation.

Concessions Manager Al Friedlander and his assistant, Pat O'Toole, were masters of their trade, and under their skilled guidance, the Browns' concessions operation was a gold mine. To this day, I firmly believe that the administrators, both in the college and professional ranks, who farm out their concessions rights to an outside vendor for thirty-five percent of the gross have done themselves and their programs a financial injustice.

From Modell, I learned the value of the electronic media as a revenue producer. In the early days of television coverage of the NFL, negotiations with the networks were pretty much left up to the individual clubs. Modell, whose background was in advertising, helped consolidate the teams, and under his expert direction, the NFL's first big television contract was signed.

Like an indulgent parent, Modell allowed me to dabble in any area which caught my childlike curiosity. There were times when my intrusion caused literal upheaval.

For instance, when I decided that the scouting combines utilized by many of the NFL clubs, the Browns included, were not worth the tremendous fees they charged, I set out to invent my own computer rating system. This system graded potential draft choices as well as the scouts who were recommending them.

After attempting, unsuccessfully, to convince then-General Manager Harold Sauerbrie of the value of my plan, I set up my own draft desk and conducted my own college draft.

My little project left Sauerbrie and the entire scouting department so mad at me that I never did reveal my draft picks. That's too bad, because several of my selections enjoyed long, illustrious careers. In fact, Tom Jackson, one of my highest rated collegians, went on to become one of the NFL's great linebackers with the Denver Broncos in a career that spanned thirteen seasons.

The years I spent with the Browns were invaluable to my training process, but the one thing they failed to teach me was patience.

In 1971, at age thirty-four, I decided I was ready to become a general manager. Unfortunately, the position in Cleveland didn't promise to be vacant any time soon.

I pursued and was offered the GM job in Houston, which had been open since Don Klosterman left the Oilers for the Baltimore Colts the year before. Once there, however, I discovered that certain promises made to me of administrative and fiscal control were not being fulfilled, and eight weeks later, I was ready to return to the real world of the NFL and leave the oil fields to the Texans.

Modell welcomed me back to the Browns with a promotion, naming me vice president and treasurer, as well as to the board of directors, although I suspected his decision to rehire me was based upon his respect for my administrative abilities. As I would come to find out, my leaving for Houston had caused irreparable damage to our personal relationship, and we would never regain the friendship we had once shared.

During this time, Modell did allow me to pursue an idea of which I remain very proud. I devised a way to build and finance a stadium to be owned and operated by the franchise, rather than the municipality in which it was located.

Sound as the idea was, however, it never came to fruition. Just weeks before the scheduled groundbreaking, Modell called the whole thing off. The only explanation I was ever given was that Modell's new wife didn't like new stadiums, and he had decided to refurbish Cleveland's Municipal Stadium, instead. Had he told me he was also going to drain Lake Erie, I would not have been more disappointed. Shortly afterwards, disillusioned by the untimely demise of the project, I left the Browns for good.

In 1974, I went to work for a powerful Phoenix businessman, Karl Eller, who was the driving force behind a move to secure an NFL expansion franchise for that city. With the promise of the general manager's job if the team came to pass, I worked for five months to secure a lease arrangement with Arizona State University for the use of Sun Devil Stadium.

In the end, the NFL Selection Committee turned thumbs down on Phoenix, awarding the coveted franchises to Seattle and Tampa Bay, instead.

Back home in Cleveland, I decided to return one of the several telephone calls which had been made to me by John Bassett of the new World Football League. The WFL was coming off a disastrous inaugural season, marred by the undisciplined signing of current, as well as over-the-hill, NFL players for ridiculous sums of money, and I had serious reservations regarding the viability of the league. But I considered Bassett an astute businessman and was curious to hear what he had to say.

Bassett managed to pique my interest with a description of an intelligent new financial formula the league had just adopted. The Hemmeter Plan, named after its author and new WFL President Chris Hemmeter, called for most players to be paid one percent of their team's gate receipts each week, or $500 per game, whichever was greater. I thought the plan had merit, and agreed to meet with Hemmeter and Bassett to discuss it further.

In early 1975, I was invited to attend a league meeting in Memphis. It was there that I was offered the job of president and general manager of the new Portland, Ore., franchise, the Thunder.

I arrived in Portland on April 1, 1975, briefcase in hand. The season would begin in early August, which meant I had four months to form a management group, assemble a coaching staff and sign enough players to field a football team.

My task was not made any easier by the fact that the 1974 Portland franchise, the Storm, had walked away without paying about $1 million worth of bills.

Despite the fact that the Thunder was a totally separate entity from the Storm, the city of Portland had been left with a bad taste in its mouth, and our attendance figures reflected it. I quickly became a master of deficit financing.

Several weeks into the season, it was apparent that the Thunder was faring no better on the field, and I decided that a coaching change might be necessary.

Greg Barton, at age twenty-eight, was the youngest head coach in professional football history. He had played quarterback for the Storm the previous year, and seemed to be having difficulty disciplining his former teammates, some of whom were older than he was.

After the Thunder lost its fifth game of the season (against one victory), I fired Barton, and for a lack of anything resembling common sense, named myself interim head coach.

My first game as coach was against the Philadelphia Bell in Philadelphia. I had played in a lot of football games over the years, but I can't recall ever being as scared before any of them as I was before that one. In fact, the team doctor had to give me a Valium in the locker room before the team took the field. If he hadn't, I probably would have had a heart attack on the sidelines.

When the gun sounded, the Thunder had won its second game of the season, 25-10, and I had developed a complete and utter respect for the coaching profession.

The following week brought the powerful Memphis

Southmen to town. This team featured the league's best record as well as the Terrific Trio: former Miami Dolphins Larry Csonka, Jim Kiick and Paul Warfield. When they and their teammates headed back to Tennessee, I was 1-1 as a head coach.

I decided that if I was going to avert a nervous breakdown, I needed to hire a coach, and I brought in Joe Gardi from the Philadelphia Bell. Gardi's Thunder debut would take place on October 4, 1975, against the Jacksonville Express in the Gator Bowl. Unfortunately, he would coach his first game under less-than-ideal circumstances. The Thunder had seventeen players on injured reserve, and thanks to our financial problems, there weren't enough payroll funds to replace them.

With twenty-eight men, many of them playing both ways and on the special teams, as well, the Thunder staged one of the most courageous performances I'd ever seen. With just minutes remaining in the game, and the score at 32-29 in favor of the Express, the team mounted a final drive for the end zone. When it stalled on the ten-yard line, Gardi called a time-out. A field goal would tie the game and send it into overtime.

To my horror, Gardi sent the offense back onto the field. "What's he doing?" I screamed from the press box. "What is going on down there?"

Don Horn took the snap from center and dropped back to pass. His receiver, Jim Thorpe, broke free from coverage and turned for the ball. He turned the wrong way, however, and the pass fell incomplete. I almost fell out of the press box.

After the game, I couldn't get to the locker room quickly enough, and I stormed through the door in search of Gardi. Before I could utter a word, he winked at me and said, "Twenty-eight guys gave it all they had, boss." Gardi had gone for the win because he knew the players had given everything they had. There was nothing left for an overtime.

Two-and-a-half weeks later, the WFL had nothing left, either, and on October 22, 1975, the league ceased operations.

After the hurt wore off, I was left with a feeling of deep disappointment. I had followed the Hemmeter Plan religiously, and believed the league could have survived. Such was not to be.

As we closed the doors for the last time, I was most proud that the Thunder's owners lost only their original investments and were not subjected to the countless lawsuits filed by players and unpaid vendors in WFL cities across the country. In fact, the Portland Thunder was to go down in history as the only "successful failure" of the defunct World Football League.

Suddenly out of work, with a hefty house note and 2,500 miles from Cleveland, which, after just a year in Portland, we still considered home, I had to find gainful employment. In a hurry. I went to work on an hourly basis for a Portland CPA firm, and Kay took a part-time job as a nursery school teacher. I kept my ear to the ground for an entree back into the NFL, and we made do.

In the meantime, I heard that the Athletic Director's job at the University of Oregon was vacant, and I applied. I had no burning desire to enter the world of intercollegiate athletics. I just needed a well-paying job.

I survived the first several rounds of eliminatory cuts, and I found myself being invited for an interview. When asked why I thought the Athletic Department had experienced financial difficulties to that point, I bluntly answered, "Because there has been a lack of funds due to the previous administration's inability to run the department like a business."

I think I scared the university's president half to death. Mentioning commercialism within the hallowed halls of ivy bordered, it appeared by his reaction, on blasphemy. I didn't get the job.

By that point, I was becoming a little nervous, and I was suddenly in the position to consider, and ultimately accept, a job offer made by a friend of mine who had played some years back for the Washington Redskins. Walt Houston owned a nail manufacturing company in Cleveland, Angell Nail Company, which was in need of management expertise. He offered me the job of president, and I was out of sports for the first time in my professional life.

A nail is a nail is a nail . . .

Running a nail manufacturing company taxes one's marketing abilities, not to mention patience, to the fullest, and the years I spent at its helm were trying times, indeed. The company did manage to make money, despite two labor strikes, but I deeply missed professional sports, and hoped every day for the phone call which would invite me back.

My contacts within the NFL were friendly enough, but nothing materialized. It seems that my stint in the WFL had branded me as a renegade, and it would be five long years before that label wore off.

Finally, Mike Robbie, the general manager of the Miami Dolphins and son of owner Joe Robbie, called to invite me to Miami for an interview.

I was to meet with the elder Robbie on a Saturday, and I flew in from Cleveland early that morning. The meeting never came off, however. It seems that Robbie, who knew I was waiting to see him, got sidetracked, and I returned to Cleveland both confused and disillusioned over the weekend's events.

The following week, Mike called to set up another meeting between his father and me. On this trip, I did, in fact, sit down with the owner of the Dolphins, and after some intensive negotiations, was offered the job of director of finances.

I worked very hard during my stay with the Dolphins to become a communications conduit between the Robbie-ruled front office and the football operation, run just as possessively by Head Coach Don Shula. The well-chronicled differences between the men, two of the most powerful in the NFL, made it a precarious position in which to be. It would take all the diplomatic skills I could muster to survive those two years.

During the spring of 1982, Dr. Joe Hoy, then the director of the Sports Administration program at Biscayne College in Miami, invited me to speak at a seminar on job opportunities in the field of sports administration. At the end of my speech, Hoy asked me if I had ever given any thought to a career in college athletics. I told him I had never given it much consideration, my University of Oregon experience notwithstanding, but that I might if the right situation presented itself.

A few days later, Hoy called to tell me that the Athletic Director's job at Louisiana State University would soon be vacant, and that I ought to give some thought to applying.

The only thing I knew about LSU was that in 1958, my Duke Blue Devils had travelled to Baton Rouge to meet the Tigers and their great tailback, Billy Cannon. I liked to tell people that at one point, Duke led 6-0 against the eventual national champions. I usually forgot to mention that the final score was 50-18, LSU.

Hoy had some sketchy information regarding the job, including the fact that Athletic Director Paul Dietzel was being reassigned within the university system and that a search committee had been formed to find his replacement. His source also told him that the LSU Athletic Department was deeply submerged in red ink and that future projections were for more of the same.

Hoy said he had called the university to ask for information regarding the search procedure and had spoken with Chancellor James Wharton. Wharton, in turn, had referred him to the head of the search committee, Dr. Charlie Roberts, who recommended to Hoy that I give him a call.

I called Roberts the next day, and he asked me to submit a resume to the university as quickly as possible. He told me to be sure to include a list of personal references. He gave me a brief overview of the job, and his enthusiasm was contagious. I found my interest mounting.

I quickly prepared a letter-type resume and sent it on its way, along with a request that my application be kept secret, since I felt certain that Robbie would not take kindly to one of his employees seeking a job elsewhere.

Just as quickly, Roberts called and asked me to come to Baton Rouge. He told me he wanted me to meet with some of the key people involved in the selection process. I told him I'd be happy to visit, but, once again, I wanted to be assured of confidentiality. He promised I would be, and I booked my own flight into New Orleans. Roberts was to meet me at the airport.

During the hour-plus drive from New Orleans to Baton Rouge, Roberts filled me in on the details of the Athletic Director's job. I found him to be extremely knowledgeable about the position. He was also a veritable walking encyclopedia when it came to any dirt he could attribute to Dietzel and his four-year administration.

Arriving in Baton Rouge, I registered at the Hilton, then had dinner with a few of Roberts' key people. Afterwards, I was whisked back to the hotel to wait while Roberts made a quick trip to the Chancellor's house to report in.

It wasn't long before Roberts returned to the hotel and told me that he had recommended to the Chancellor that they call off the search. As far as Roberts was concerned, he told me, they had found their man. Simple as that.

No bells went off. No sirens blazed. I had just been swept, quickly and painlessly, into the world of LSU politics. And I hadn't felt a thing.

On the way to the New Orleans airport the next day, Roberts told me that if I was really interested in the position, he would handle everything on the Baton Rouge end. I was simply to sit back and remain undercover until the interview process was completed. That process, I was told, would begin the following Monday and would include ten applicants.

I found it a little strange, after having been told by Roberts that I fit the bill, that the search committee would go through the motions of interviewing ten applicants. But, then again, I'd never been involved in college athletics, and I assumed that this must be the way it was done. I returned home to Miami and excitedly told Kay that our chances of getting the job looked very, very good.

I can only guess as to what transpired in Baton Rouge over the course of the next two weeks. I returned to the Dolphins' front office and entrusted my fate to Roberts. I didn't know at the time that I couldn't have picked a more capable guardian.

In retrospect, I don't know how Roberts and Wharton convinced the LSU Board of Supervisors that I was the man for the job. I had three strikes against me. I was a Yankee, I was from the pro ranks with no college experience and I had no ties to LSU. In fact, I would become the first Athletic Director in the fifty-year history of the position with no prior LSU affiliation.

Several weeks passed before I received my official invitation to be interviewed by the search committee. Fearful that Robbie's suspicions might be aroused by my second absense from Miami in less than a month, I once again voiced my concerns to Roberts. He assured me that there was nothing to worry about. The job, he told me, was in the bag.

I arrived in Baton Rouge, and spent an entire day going through the motions of a formal interview with the search committee. I have always wondered if my questioners really believed they had any say in the selection of the new Athletic Director, or if they were simply putting up an awfully good front.

When the interview was over, Roberts offered me the job, and we negotiated my salary. I wanted $72,000 a year, but Roberts told me that it would be to my advantage, given the starting salaries of LSU professors and other department heads, to start at under $70,000. We settled on $69,500.

I was willing to accept less than what I wanted for two reasons: One, Roberts told me that as an employee of the state of Louisiana, I could expect annual raises of between seven and ten percent; and two, he described to me an Athletic Department discretionary fund that he said would be at my disposal.

The "LSA Fund," as he called it, contained $30,000. It could be used to pay for such things as country club dues and any number of entertainment-related expenses which, according to state law, the university was prohibited from covering. Roberts told me that it had been in existence for some thirty years and that I would assume control sometime after taking the job.

I left for Miami, assured by Roberts that my next trip to Baton Rouge would be to appear before the Board of Supervisors on confirmation day, Friday, May 21, 1982.

I made another trip to Baton Rouge before that time, however. This one was for the purpose of giving Kay and my son, Jason, a firsthand look at our new home. We toured the campus, checked out a few neighborhoods nearby, then ate our first batch of crawfish at a local seafood restaurant.

As we returned to the hotel for the evening, Jason said to me, "I am really excited about this job, Dad."

He was genuinely looking forward to living in Baton Rouge, and I was touched by his sincerity.

"So am I, son. So am I."

Kay and I flew into Baton Rouge on Thursday, May 20, under the names Mr. and Mrs. Robert Kaye. Roberts hid us that night at his home, and expressed great glee at putting one over on the local media, whom he said would be checking the airports and hotels for Robert and Kay Brodhead.

That evening, Roberts also informed me that when I appeared before the Board the next day, its members would be asking me a few questions. He carefully coached me on what to expect, gave me a complete biography of each Board member and made a number of suggestions as to the way I should answer specific questions.

I was beginning to feel the first needlings of apprehension. It was evident that tomorrow's Board meeting was going to entail a lot more than the routine confirmation I had expected. What would happen, I wondered to myself, if the Board didn't share Roberts' conviction that I be hired?

Shortly before noon on Friday, Kay and I were taken to the LSU Systems Building, where we were to wait while the Chancellor made his formal recommendation to the Board that I be hired.

I had left my letter of resignation, addressed to Joe Robbie, with a Miami courier service. Upon word from me, my secretary would notify the courier to deliver the letter to the Dolphins' offices. As the afternoon wore on and Kay and I sat nervously in the Systems Building waiting room, I hoped the letter hadn't been delivered prematurely.

Finally, the Board announced that it would go into executive session to interview me, and I came face to face with the people Roberts had told me so much about. For eighty minutes, I answered a variety of questions and offered a number of my philosophies on athletics as a whole, and when the vote was taken, I was confirmed by a margin of 13-1 as the sixth Athletic Director of Louisiana State University.

The lone vote of dissent was cast by Charles Cusimano of New Orleans. It seems I had managed to make my first enemy at LSU in a little less than an afternoon.

In my acceptance speech, I pledged to the Board that "we will very quickly win again in football, and we will continue to win in basketball." I also told the Board members that "the time span will be short. I'm an impatient person, and I realize that the great fans of LSU are an impatient group, also."

Kay and I returned to Miami, thrilled with the opportunity we had just been handed. I considered it the greatest challenge of my career and was anxious for June 1, the day I would officially take over the Athletic Department, to arrive. Little did I know that during the next four-and-a-half years, I would encounter a variety of dark forces, ranging from campus politics to an FBI sting operation, from State Ethics Commission investigations to betrayal.

The next day, I received a phone call at my home from Jerry Stovall, Head Coach of the LSU Tigers football team. He had called, he announced, to voice his displeasure over my statements to the Board about winning immediately.

Welcome to LSU.

CHAPTER TWO

Red Ink
and Missing Ribeyes

My job as Athletic Director of Louisiana State University officially began on June 1, 1982.

My predecessor, Paul Dietzel, had exited following the end of the 1981 fiscal year when a Legislative audit requested by Louisiana State Senator B.B. "Sixty" Rayburn and an internal audit undertaken simultaneously had uncovered a $1.4 million deficit in the Athletic Department.

I had been sent an official copy of the audit report to review while I wrapped up loose ends in Miami. Having been preconditioned by the emphatic accounts put forth by Chancellor Jim Wharton and his administrative assistant, Charlie Roberts, describing Dietzel's alleged mismanagement, I fully expected to find a financial horror story on every report page.

As I studied the report, however, my auditing background told me that much of the content of these voluminous audit work papers was devoted to nothing more than "boiler plate" items. Like the audits of any number of corporations, the LSU Athletic Department audit had produced the clichéd findings and subsequent suggestions that occur time and time again in reviews of internal control. In most instances, the majority of these items are deemed impractical, if not impossible, to implement by the audited corporation, and only those which will protect it against cash fraud and other breakdowns of internal control are utilized.

Also contained within the audit report were a number of items which my experienced eye judged immaterial, unless they had been included for the purpose of discrediting someone.

By the time I finished my review, it was clear that the Administration's finding of "mismanagement" on Dietzel's part was not based upon the discovery of fraudulent business practices undertaken by Dietzel, but upon its narrow interpretation of the report's content. Nowhere was there proof of any fraud perpetrated by Dietzel, nor would I find any evidence of such during my four-and-a-half-year tenure at LSU.

Like the rest of the public, I had been sold a bill of goods regarding Dietzel's Athletic Department.

This is not to say that Dietzel was a good administrator. He was not. What he was was a magnificently talented football coach and fine recruiter who had been thrust into the world of business where, like many in similar situations, he floundered. Academic administrators have never learned that coaching excellence is rarely an indication of administrative expertise.

Dietzel failed to recognize and utilize the limitless sources of potential revenue available to LSU's Athletic Department, and his long-term budget had projected the loss of considerable amounts of money over the ensuing four years.

The following summary is taken from his projections:

FISCAL YEAR	PROJECTED LOSS
1982-83	$ (759,414)
1983-84	(467,790)
1984-85	(1,372,015)
1985-86	(1,175,909)
TOTAL	$(3,775,128)

The financial future of Dietzel's Athletic Department

was bleak, indeed. Yet there was no way to determine, by reading the audit report, which of the business practices responsible for the projected deficit were of Dietzel's design and which had been inherited by Dietzel from his predecessors. Particularly since the audit of the Athletic Department was the first in its fifty-year history.

It was my opinion that Dietzel's downfall as an administrator was his reliance on Assistant Athletic Director Larry Jones, a former LSU football player and coach, to perform administrative functions which were far beyond the poor man's capabilities. When the internal audit uncovered doctored expense vouchers which had been submitted by coaches and members of the administrative staff, it was Jones, not Dietzel, who had approved the majority of them. Yet it was Dietzel, not Jones, who lost his job. I would inherit, at the Administration's request, Larry Jones as an assistant athletic director. The Chancellor would get a pipeline.

Dietzel's greatest sin was delegating authority to others. Sadly, the others in question were no more capable of doing the job than he was. The job they ultimately did was on him.

Arriving on campus, I did find several things which the auditors had not included in their report: an Athletic Department shredded by disloyalty from within; rampant paranoia; constant interference by the Chancellor; a host of hand-picked informants who reported directly, and regularly, to Wharton and Roberts; the relegation of "the minor sports," a label worn by everything but football and basketball, to second-class citizen status; and a mad scramble by department personnel to find a niche in the Chancellor's power group. Judas would have felt right at home on the LSU campus.

The worst of my findings was the nagging feeling that the internal audit had not been ordered to uncover problems within the Athletic Department and make suggestions to help solve them; it had been ordered to find fault with Paul

Dietzel. The result of the purge was a fragmented, disjointed Athletic Department with all of its pre-audit problems intact. It appeared to me that I was looking at a tragic case of missing the forest for the sake of a tree.

Ironically, the audit had failed to look closely at the two areas which are most vulnerable to fraud within the sports industry: concessions and ticket sales. Both are cash-and-carry business functions where money is readily accessible and, therefore, difficult to control. As such, both areas should have been audited regularly, and in depth.

The infrequently performed audits of the Athletic Department's ticket office had apparently been superficial in nature. For example, if the amount of cash on deposit had corresponded with the value of the tickets sold for the period in question, all was assumed to be in order. Given the enormous number of transactions and amount of cash involved in athletic ticket sales, however, cursory audits performed by those unfamiliar with the sports industry generally proved to be inadequate.

My personal audit of the Athletic Department's ticket office raised two questions: Number one, why did the records reflect such a large number of football tickets being sold on a single-game basis when there was a waiting list years long of people wanting to purchase season tickets?

I suspected that someone was selling the seats as season tickets, recording them as single-game sales and pocketing the $10-per-season-ticket surcharge. The buyers must have been willing to hazard that "underground" season tickets were better than none at all. The university, it appeared, was getting the short end of the stick, losing out on approximately $40,000 a year in surcharge revenues.

The following season, I confiscated the 4,000 seats in question and put them on sale to the general public on a season-ticket basis. A lot of people who thought they'd never see a season ticket were elated; the seats' former owners were something else.

I must assume, however, that had these folks believed I had divested them of their legitimately held season tickets, I would have faced a tidal wave of opposition. What I got was an undercurrent of dissension. In fact, I've often wondered if some of the animosity shown towards me by certain high-ranking university officials, as well as a select group of Baton Rouge businessmen, couldn't be tied directly to the drying up of this viable ticket source.

Question number two: How was it that not one of LSU's 50,000-plus season tickets was ever lost by attrition? Assuming, conservatively, that six to eight percent of season ticket holders move away, die or simply do not renew their seats, there should have been 3,000 to 4,000 season tickets appearing on the non-renewal list at the end of each football season. Logic would dictate that a percentage of these would be prime seats. There were none. Why not?

It would take me four years to find the answer to that question, which I will disclose in a later chapter.

Potential problem area number two, concessions, had been subjected to even fewer audits than had the ticket office: none. This was the case, I was told, because concessions at LSU had always been handled by an outside vendor.

LSU's contract with its concessionaire was fairly standard, calling for the university to receive between thirty-eight and forty percent of gross concessions sales. When I examined the dollars-and-cents figures representing this percentage, however, it was apparent that something had been lost in the translation.

I had been deeply involved in the internal concessions operations of both the Cleveland Browns and the Miami Dolphins, and my experiences had taught me well. I knew all about per capita concessions averages and attendance formula projections. That's why it was obvious to me that LSU was suffering from a bad case of "the shorts."

Armed with my findings and a long-held belief that concessions are best handled internally, I proposed that the Athletic Department assume control of this function. Why should the university part with its concessions rights for a forty-percent return when, by handling its own, it stood to make a profit of double or even triple that amount?

It shouldn't, but that seemed obvious to me alone, judging by the resistance my suggestion generated. I would have to prove to the skeptics the merit of my idea, and I called upon the aid of the best man in the business, Orange Bowl Concessions Manager Pat O'Toole.

Using a few trusted employees, we infiltrated the ranks of LSU's concessionaire and discovered a subtle skimming operation involving up to twenty percent of the gross receipts from certain stadium concessions stands. Enlisting the cooperation of the local Coca-Cola distributor, we also discovered how Coke sales were being manipulated as a part of this scheme by an outside supplier. Empty Coke syrup containers, which should have been used to determine the number of Cokes sold during the course of a game, were being refilled with bootleg Coke syrup early on Sunday morning before a container count could be made.

The discrepancy between the actual number of Cokes sold and the number reported as sold based upon the supposedly unopened Coke syrup containers was tremendous.

O'Toole and I also suspected there might be problems with a number of individual concessions stands, in particular, several which had been manned for years by nonprofit organizations in return for a percentage of those stands' gross sales. While there is nothing wrong with this practice — in fact, it's a rather civic-minded thing to do — it could not be allowed to occur without supervision.

We managed to get our hands on the sales sheets from enough of these stands to determine that they had, indeed, been allowed to operate with little or no accountability for the monies they collected. Many of the sales sheets were blatantly out of balance, and I was amazed at this obvious lack of control.

As closely as I could estimate, LSU was losing in excess of $200,000 per annum through the concessions windows as a result of inaccurate stand reports, understated Coke sales and otherwise shoddy bookkeeping practices. How long it had been going on was anybody's guess, but I couldn't help but wonder how so many problem areas had gone undetected when, during the course of the internal audit, the amount of coffee consumed by Athletic Department personnel had been investigated and deemed excessive.

By the time O'Toole and I were through, the evidence we had accumulated was so overwhelming that any resistance to assuming control of concessions had disappeared.

Another of the problems awaiting me in Baton Rouge was Broussard Hall, the ancient dormitory which houses LSU's scholarship athletes. Shortly after I arrived, I began to receive complaints from Broussard employees concerning the way in which the facility was being run. The most disturbing grievance I heard was that management was stealing food from the Broussard kitchen. Management responsibility for Broussard Hall fell to Larry Jones, whom I discovered was employing two of his sons at the facility, in direct conflict with university policy.

I commenced yet another personal investigation, and when I reviewed Broussard's most recent cost-of-food-served figures, I found a number of troublesome disparities, so I immediately asked that a physical inventory be taken. Neither the Department of Business Affairs nor the university internal auditors would respond to my requests.

Finally, after several months had passed and I had resorted to making threats of varying degrees, a count was made, and a shortage of approximately $10,000 was found. Given the limited scope of the investigation, I knew even that was a conservative estimate.

The biggest disappearing act had been performed by 1,600 pounds of prime ribeye steaks, enough meat for seven meals for the football team or fourteen meals for the "minor sports" teams. (Allow me to explain here that before I arrived at LSU, football players were served the big steaks while everyone else ate the smaller ones.)

If I was amazed by the results of the inventory, I was dumbfounded by the university's official reaction to them. The woman accountable for the shortages was granted a sick leave and, a year later, was reassigned to another position within the university system.

Another of my personal findings was a "slush fund" which existed for the discretionary use of the football coaching staff. Money for this fund was being provided, I discovered, through the sale of football tickets which had been earmarked for recruiting purposes and for purchase by jobbers, those local businessmen who employ scholarship athletes during the summer months.

Because these tickets were lumped together under one category heading, there were no detailed records kept of their purchase. As a result, each one was being sold for $1,000 above its face value. During particularly profitable sales years, the slush fund was said to contain in excess of $80,000.

From what I could gather, these transactions had been going on for years, and the list of secret customers would often read like a "Who's Who" in Baton Rouge. I tried to put an end to the practice as quickly as possible.

During the course of the audit, two deficiencies had been found pertaining to the management of the LSU Radio Network. One, signed contracts with football broadcast advertisers were nowhere to be found, and two, the sale of advertising time had not been booked as accounts receivable. In fact, the only records kept regarding the sale of advertising time were those made when a payment was received. Records of delinquent accounts, some of which were as many as three years past due, did not exist.

To determine the amount of advertising revenue still unaccounted for, the auditors had listened to tapes of game broadcasts and counted the number of ad minutes they found. They then queried John Ferguson, who not only provided "The Voice of the Tigers," but also sold the advertising in question. At the end of their investigation, they recommended the booking of more than $50,000 as due and owing the university.

After that, not much more was said on the subject, but I wasn't quite ready to see the case closed. Something about the telephone company's line fees had struck me as odd, and curiosity led me to review the charges. What I found was that each broadcast had actually begun thirty minutes prior to kickoff time and had run another thirty or so minutes beyond the game's conclusion. In all instances, the university had remitted the amount due without so much as a question as to what had transpired during that extra hour of each broadcast.

The tapes themselves offered no insight, since they contained only the calls of the actual games. But some investigative auditing revealed that many stations along the line had been invoiced for pre- and post-game shows. Strangely, the billings were written on plain white stationery, and the return address was a post office box.

There was no way to determine whether or not advertising had been sold on these segments. If it had, and I strongly suspected as much, records of such transactions were not in evidence.

At this time, I also began to review all Athletic Department expenditures which had been made during the years in which a deficit had been recorded. I had inherited more than a million dollars worth of red ink, and if I was going to eradicate it, I would need every bit of information I could get my hands on.

I started with one of the areas which had seen more than its fair share of Athletic Department money: stadium operations and maintenance. By tracing the flow of paperwork from the vendors' original invoices to the stadium work orders which required the approval of an Athletic Department employee, I hoped to pinpoint where some of the money was going. I did. And I didn't like it.

Not only were many of these work orders loaded with doctored hours, they were full of names which must have been borrowed from a bad version of the boardgame Clue.

How many Barry Bolts or Wally Washers or Fred Faucets do you know?

To this day, I can't image how such a crudely disguised sham managed to go unnoticed by an audit that would become the decisive factor in the firing of several people and the restriction of several more.

The single year's worth of phony work orders I pinned down contained approximately $50,000 in billings, which the university had paid.

I immediately alerted the Chancellor and the Department of Business Affairs to my findings. An internal investigation was ordered, but I was never notified as to its findings. The Chancellor reportedly took some sort of punitive action against the employee who had approved the work orders, but since he had already been transferred out of the Athletic Department, I was unable to verify that, as well. If a reprimand was, in fact, administered, it probably never made its way into the employee's personnel file, given the fact that he is now employed in the Athletic Department of another university.

I had been an auditor with Haskins & Sells for five years. During that period of time, I investigated more types of business establishments than I knew existed, and I uncovered more bogus business practices than I cared to believe were possible. But I had never seen a more financially corrupt situation than the one I had walked into at LSU.

While neither the Legislative audit nor the internal audit had uncovered the real problems facing the Athletic Department, my personal investigations had. And one way or the other, I intended to fix them.

CHAPTER THREE

"Are You Wearing A Bulletproof Vest?"

I am convinced that one of the primary reasons I was hired by LSU was to fire Head Football Coach Jerry Stovall.

Named head coach prior to the start of the 1980 football season, Stovall was arguably the most popular athlete to come out of LSU over the past fifty years. As an offensive halfback and defensive safety for the 1959-62 Tigers, Stovall earned a number of impressive distinctions, including All-SEC in 1961 and '62 and SEC Player of the Year, unanimous All-America and Heisman Trophy runner-up in 1962.

Stovall, who was born in the northern Louisiana town of West Monroe, was drafted in the first round by the NFL's St. Louis Cardinals. He played nine seasons, 1963-71, and was named to the Pro Bowl in 1966 and 1967.

In Stovall's inaugural season as coach of the Tigers, the team finished 7-4. The following season, Tiger fans suffered through the worst record posted by an LSU football team in the past quarter-century: 3-7-1.

Not known for its collective patience, the Administration had quickly grown tired of the roller coaster ride. But it was aware of Stovall's popularity and was reluctant to involve itself in the controversy that firing him was sure to cause.

Whoever relieved Stovall of his coaching duties would undoubtedly incur the wrath of a large regiment of north Louisiana fans as well as that of a powerful group of Baton Rouge businessmen who had grown accustomed to the top-shelf treatment they received as long as their man was in the cat-bird seat.

And so, caught between the proverbial rock and a hard place, the Administration had sought to hire an Athletic Director who, number one, was an experienced businessman capable of restoring order to the financially decimated Athletic Department; two, was capable of making tough decisions in a timely manner; and three, was a knowledgeable football person who could ultimately pull the plug on the popular Stovall.

Enter Bob Brodhead.

When Stovall called me at my home in Florida to express his views on my "we will win immediately" remarks to the Board of Supervisors, I knew there would be trouble in Red Stick city.

As I would soon find out, the football coach at LSU had historically ruled the roost, making all decisions relevant to his program. Former Athletic Director Carl Maddox was once overheard to say that he was Athletic Director of everything *but* football. Judging by my phone conversation with Stovall, he obviously hoped the new A.D. would continue the tradition.

Before I had set a foot on the LSU campus, the local press was predicting a head-on confrontation between the Head Coach and the "brash Miamian" who had dared to question the Athletic Department's sacred cow, football.

Despite the predictions, I didn't hit town looking for a fight with Stovall. On the contrary. I had been handed two mandates by the Board of Supervisors upon accepting the job, and I needed Stovall's help to accomplish the one that read, "Make the LSU Athletic Department competitive." I was simply asking of Stovall what I would of all my coaches. He was to win.

As the 1982 season began, that's exactly what he did.

The Tigers rolled over Oregon State, 45-7, and Rice, 52-13, on consecutive weekends in late September, then went on the road and knocked off the nation's fourth-ranked team, the Florida Gators, 24-13.

When the Tennessee Volunteers scored ten points in the final ten minutes to tie the Tigers at home, I heard the faint rumblings of unrest from Tiger fans who hadn't forgotten, despite the terrific start to this season, the 3-7-1 aberration of the previous year.

The team came back with three impressive performances against Kentucky, South Carolina and Mississippi to up its record to 6-0-1, then handed the Alabama Crimson Tide what Coach Paul "Bear" Bryant called "the best beating we've had since the '60s," 20-10, in Birmingham.

Not since 1970 had an LSU team defeated the Crimson Tide, but on that brilliant November afternoon, the Tigers outclassed Bryant's charges to end what LSU quarterback Alan Risher aptly called "twelve years of suffering."

The following week, LSU was scheduled to meet the Mississippi State Bulldogs in Starkville, Miss. Up until game time, the country's major bowl games were expressing an abundance of interest in the sixth-ranked Tigers. This had become a point of contention between Stovall and me, since the Executive Director of the Bluebonnet Bowl, who happened to be a close personal friend of Stovall's, was exerting pressure on the Coach to commit to a post-season appearance in Houston. Stovall, in turn, was applying the pressure on me to formally accept the invitation.

As long as such major bowls as the Orange, Gator and Liberty were interested, however, I was not about to commit to the Bluebonnet, which not only paid its participants far less money than the bigger bowls but was, at that time, without network TV coverage. I made my stance very clear to Stovall.

Awaiting kickoff in Starkville, I was exchanging the customary pleasantries in the press box when Sports Information Director Paul Manasseh appeared in the doorway, ashen-faced. He grabbed my arm, nearly dragged me into the men's room, locked the door and began ranting about what he'd just witnessed.

Stovall, Manasseh said, had issued an ultimatum to the Orange Bowl committeemen visiting the team in the locker room that if the Orange Bowl wanted LSU, it should be willing to do what the Bluebonnet Bowl was prepared to do — issue their invitation here and now, before the team took the field.

The Orange Bowl representatives did not take kindly to this approach and let Manasseh know, in no uncertain terms, that as far as they were concerned, the Tigers could spend New Year's Day in Baton Rouge. The fact that the team went out and lost 27-24 to the underdog Bulldogs didn't help matters any.

Back in Baton Rouge, I spent all day Sunday on the telephone, trying desperately to make amends with the Orange Bowl. My best shot at salvaging the situation appeared to be in working a deal with the Orange Bowl and the Gator Bowl involving the Tigers' next opponent, seventh-ranked Florida State. Both bowls were expressing a great deal of interest in the powerful Seminoles, and the Gator Bowl was willing to gamble that the Tigers would also be an attractive choice. After some intensive negotiations with the Orange Bowl reps, the deal was consummated. The winner of the LSU-FSU game would be in Miami on January 1 for the Orange Bowl; the loser would get a trip to the Gator Bowl in Jacksonville.

ABC Television, figuring the game carried significant bowl ramifications, wanted it for its national game of the week and called to ask me if I would move the starting time up eight hours, to 11:30 a.m., to allow the network to carry the game. Tough as it was to turn down the $100,000 national television spot, I declined. I didn't want to do anything to disrupt the team's momentum. The game was far too important to the future of the football program.

Florida State Athletic Director C.W. "Hootie" Ingram and Football Coach Bobby Bowden didn't appreciate my line of thinking. Because FSU was an independent and didn't have to split its TV take with fellow conference members, it stood to gain $500,000 from the network deal. Ingram offered to wrestle me at halftime on the mid-field stripe. Bowden said he'd put his money on Ingram.

Florida State brought an 8-1 record and a powerful offense into Tiger Stadium on the night of November 20. The students brought oranges, every orange from every super-market within a fifty-mile radius of campus.

When the final gun sounded, LSU had to its credit one of the most impressive victories in Tiger Stadium history, 55-21. In the victor's locker room following the game, the Tigers were officially invited to meet the Nebraska Corn-huskers in the January 1, 1983, Orange Bowl. Out on the field, oranges flew like snowballs.

As thrilled as I was with the team's performance, I was also very proud that I had been able to patch things up with the Orange Bowl people after Stovall's blunder. As a private reminder of my efforts in negotiating the bowl deal, I truly wanted a game ball. Stovall refused, saying tradition dictated that the coaches determined who received game balls. And to prove his point, Stovall awarded one to Manasseh "for every-thing he had done to help the team receive this great honor."

The confrontation over the bowl game was the only serious dispute that Stovall and I would have. Even that, I suspected, had resulted from the resentment he felt over the fact that for the first time in a long, long time, the Athletic Director, not the Football Coach, was in charge.

LSU had one last opponent to face on its 1982 regular-season schedule, its most bitter rival, Tulane University. The seventh-ranked Tigers were a twenty-four-point favorite against the 3-7 Green Wave, but Coach Vince Gibson's bunch of rag-tags obviously hadn't read the latest line. When the dust settled, Tulane owned the biggest upset of the year, 31-28.

For some time, I had been experiencing doubts about Stovall's ability to make adjustments to his game plan once play was under way. The Tulane game reinforced my suspi-cions. In fact, had I realized then that the Tulane game was to be a preview of many such nights to come during 1983, it would have been a long off-season.

New Year's night in Miami was a pleasant experience, for three-and-a-half quarters. The Tigers hung tough with a powerful Nebraska squad, leading 17-7 late in the third period, before a Cornhusker surge resulted in a 21-20 final score.

When the final AP poll of the season was issued, the Tigers had claimed the eleventh spot.

Along with the invitation to a major bowl, the first since 1973, the brightest spot to emerge out of the '82 season was Mack Brown. One of the best young minds in football, Brown called the offensive plays and helped Alan Risher pass his way into the LSU record books. Brown was liked by both the players and press, and his popularity seemed a source of irritation to Stovall.

Brown left LSU at the end of the 1982 season, despite my best efforts to dissuade him, to become Head Football Coach at Appalachian State University in Boone, N.C. In the last conversation he and I had while he was at LSU, Brown told me the reason he was leaving was that he knew a Brodhead-Stovall blow-up was inevitable, and he didn't want to get caught in the backlash.

I was sorry to see him go. Had he stayed and continued to produce the results he had in '82, I probably would have named him Head Coach of the Tigers when I fired Stovall following the 1983 season.

Prior to the 1983 season, recruiting and spring practice went fairly smoothly, although there seemed to be an unrest among the players which, I learned, stemmed from an incident at the Orange Bowl. It seemed that several players had been caught breaking a team rule and were severely reprimanded, although the guilty "scrubs" were censored to a greater degree than the "name players" caught in the same scheme. I also learned that the seniors had taken a secret vote before the Orange Bowl game and had decided not to play unless punishment was administered equally.

As a result, the players — all of them — were forgiven their transgressions, but this would not be the last I would hear of the existence of a double standard on Stovall's football team.

Also during the off-season, Stovall requested an extension on the two years left on his contract. Being a firm believer that contracts were extended only as a reward for monumental achievement, I opted to give Stovall a substantial raise, instead. Despite the successes of the Orange Bowl season, I had a few lingering doubts regarding Stovall's coaching abilities, and I wanted another year to watch him in action.

While all contract negotiations with Stovall were left to me, with no attempts at interference by the Administration, I was getting constant input from Charlie Roberts, the Chancellor's administrative assistant. Like a "Jiminy Cricket" perched on my shoulder, Roberts never missed an opportunity to call Stovall a hypocrite, and he'd laugh as he'd tell me that the Coach's "theme song" was "Drop Kick Me, Jesus, Through the Goal Posts of Life."

Actually, Stovall was just one of Roberts' favorite topics of conversation. Another was our boss, Chancellor Wharton, about whom Roberts would complain loud and long. It wasn't long after becoming Wharton's right-hand man, in fact, that Roberts had resorted to eating stomach pills like candy.

Roberts would prove most adept at perching on shoulders. I didn't realize at the time how sharp his claws were, or how deeply they cut.

The 1983 season began with a 40-35 loss to a revenge-minded Florida State squad, followed by a victory over lowly Rice, 24-10. The highlight of the season occurred in week three with a 40-14 shellacking of highly ranked PAC-10 power Washington in front of 82,390 screaming fans, the largest crowd to ever witness a game in Tiger Stadium. That record may be the only one I left behind at LSU which will never be broken. The fire marshall had assured me of that on a number of occasions.

From that high point, the team began a precipitous nosedive from which it would never recover. Wharton, for one, wasn't enjoying the ride.

Immediately following the 21-13 loss to conference foe Kentucky, which had been preceded by losses to Florida and Tennessee, Wharton ordered me to meet him in my office. Short of issuing a mandate, he made it very clear that he wanted something done to remedy the situation. I told him I wouldn't make that kind of a decision in the heat of an emotional loss, and that the most prudent course of action would be to assume an evaluation mode, assessing the performance of the coaching staff on a week-by-week basis.

Two weeks later, following a 27-24 loss to Ole Miss in Jackson, I had seen enough. I began my search for a new head coach.

The 1982 team had come within eight points of an undefeated, untied season; the 1983 edition had, to that point, won just three games. The outstanding efforts against Alabama and Florida State in 1982, and against Washington in '83, could not be reconciled with the woeful performances in 1982 against Mississippi State and Tulane, and in 1983, against the bulk of the schedule. Something was drastically wrong, and the buck stopped on the Head Coach's doorstep.

I contacted Dick Vermeil, the successful coach-turned-TV-color-analyst, through his broadcast partner, Frank Gleber. Vermeil, who had claimed burn-out when he walked away from the Philadelphia Eagles a short time earlier, wasn't interested.

I contacted Mike White of the University of Illinois through his business manager. At White's prices, I wasn't interested.

I thought about contacting University of Maryland Head Coach Bobby Ross and several other prospects when I decided to pursue a comment which had been made to me by Bill Arnsparger, Assistant Head Coach and Defensive Coordinator of the Miami Dolphins, when I left that organization in 1982. He had asked me to keep him in mind if I ever had to make a change at LSU.

After the loss to Ole Miss, I flew to Miami to talk with Arnsparger. I found him extremely receptive to the possibility of returning to the college ranks as a head coach.

I caught a late-night plane out of Miami and spent the night in the Atlanta airport before catching the early morning flight into Baton Rouge. I didn't want to take a later flight and risk running into a horde of media people at the Baton Rouge airport. There was enough speculation being bandied about in print and over the air as to who might be the next coach, and I didn't want to add fuel to the fire.

Some members of the media had blown my week-by-week evaluation stance into a full-fledged attempt by "Bottom Line Bob" to "get Jerry Stovall." One reporter wrote that Vermeil had watched the LSU-Mississippi State game from my press box. About the only thing Vermeil and my actual guest, Billy Andrews, former Cleveland Browns linebacker and Southeastern Louisiana star, had in common was the amount of ivory they both showed when smiling. Andrews, who had been a friend of mine since our days with the Browns, had not an inkling of interest in the coaching profession. But then, the local media never allowed the facts to get in the way of a good story.

When the season ended on November 24, LSU's record was a miserable 4-7. For the first time in history, the Tigers had failed to win a single conference game, finishing 0-6 in the SEC.

I recommended to the Chancellor that Stovall be fired immediately and that the Athletic Department get on with its business. To my surprise, he didn't agree. Seems he'd changed his mind in the five weeks since our meeting after the Kentucky game, when he had wanted Stovall's scalp.

The Chancellor's new strategy called for me to wait until December 2, the date of the next regularly scheduled meeting of the Board of Supervisors, when I would be required to make a formal recommendation to fire Stovall. It was a beautiful maneuver that turned what should have been an open-and-shut matter into a public debate, complete with the shredding of Bob Brodhead by the media and the powerful Stovall backers who were set to lobby the Board on the Coach's behalf.

There were just nine days between the end of the football season and the Board meeting, but that was plenty of time for me to be ridiculed, threatened and pressured. My family and I needed a police escort from the November 26 LSU-University of New Orleans basketball game in New Orleans when a group of Tiger fans, who had taunted me and shouted obscenities during the game, was seen waiting by the exit afterwards. The ringleader of that little lynching party, Al Beloit, has since served as president of the New Orleans Alumni Federation, but on that night, there he was, standing in the aisle two rows in front of my seat so I'd be sure to see the Dump Brodhead bumper stickers he so proudly wore across his back.

There were moments during those nine days when I feared that the Board might not back me, and my own job would be in jeopardy. Had I known then what I know now, I wouldn't have lost so much sleep.

The die had been cast long before that now infamous Board meeting. "Jiminy Cricket" Roberts was sitting on my shoulder with a majority vote to accept the recommendation to fire Stovall, and I was too naive to know it.

Stovall had fooled the oddsmakers in 1982 by winning big, and he had, ironically, given me the time I needed to turn around the Athletic Department's finances and solidify my position with the Board. Had he lost in 1982, and had I fired him then, I would have fulfilled my purpose in the Administration's eyes, and I wouldn't have been around for the 1983 season, either.

Before the Board meeting, Wharton and Board member Sheldon Beychok met with Governor-elect Edwin Edwards to apprise him of my pending recommendation. Not knowing how adverse public reaction might be, they wanted Edwards kept up to date and, hopefully, in the right corner. Edwards, however, wanted firsthand information, and he summoned me to a meeting in his office.

Edwards' icy blue eyes scared me almost as much as his proclamation, minutes after Wharton, Beychok and I arrived, that Stovall and I should both be fired and a combination Coach/Athletic Director be brought in.

Wondering if I'd just been axed, I offered my arguments against such a move, telling Edwards that, in my opinion, intercollegiate sports had become big business and, as such, should be run by businessmen, not football coaches. He must have seen the logic in my remarks, because at the close of the meeting, he told me to do what I thought was best, and he promised not to interfere. It was a promise he would keep throughout my tenure at LSU.

As the date of the Board meeting approached, there was a beehive of activity around town. *Tiger Rag*, the self-appointed Bible of LSU sports, published a special "Pro/Con" edition which, rather than presenting both sides of the issue, presented what amounted to a pro-Stovall/anti-Brodhead dissertation. The print on the "Stovall side" of each page was larger than the print used on the "Brodhead side." Arguments offered for keeping Stovall seemed meatier and more impressive than those put forward defending my position of firing him.

I was later told that *Tiger Rag* Publisher Steve Myers had attended and participated in sessions held by Stovall backers to mount a "Save Jerry's Job" campaign. So much for journalistic objectivity.

A rally to show support for Stovall was planned for December 1, the evening before the Board meeting, in the parking lot of Tiger Stadium. A full-page ad was purchased in the local newspaper and ran that afternoon, calling for fan participation.

The basketball team was playing the University of Washington at 7:30 p.m., and the rally was scheduled to begin at 6:15, with the hope that it would carry over into the Assembly Center once the game began.

That afternoon, a phone call was made to the Athletic

Department requesting the stadium gates be unlocked so the "tens of thousands" of expected participants would have someplace to sit. Campus security called to request that I not attend the basketball game, just in case there might be trouble.

On my drive home from the office to tell Kay we'd be watching the game on TV, I couldn't help thinking what a sad state of affairs I was embroiled in. My family and I had been asked not to attend a basketball game because campus security feared for my safety. Why? Because I was about to recommend, not for personal gain but for the ultimate good of the university I had been hired to serve, the dismissal of a football coach who had just achieved the dubious distinction of not winning a single SEC game.

The rally sputtered and fizzled even as local TV reporters huddled the thirty or so participants close for an on-camera proclamation that, "It wasn't over for Jerry yet!"

The most disturbing by-product of this wholly unnecessary episode was that my home had to be placed under round-the-clock police surveillance, and I was accompanied to work each day by Mayor Pat Screen's personal bodyguard, who would sit outside my office door, loaded handgun under his jacket.

And the sports editor of the *Times Picayune* had the nerve to call my dealings with Stovall "gorilla tactics"?

Wharton sat back and watched while the public assault on my image continued.

The Board, in the meantime, was being bombarded from all sides. A primary election could not have been any more intense than the Brodhead/Stovall run-off the Chancellor had created.

Roberts would give me a daily report as to the votes in our camp. It appeared we were never in danger of not having the votes necessary to accomplish our goal, but the Chancellor never allowed me to feel secure. He constantly reminded me of how fickle the Board could be and warned me that, at the last minute, they might change their minds.

I later was to learn how typical such a move was on

the Chancellor's part. He loved playing the role of Crisis Man, able to step into any horribly tangled situation at the eleventh hour and, with a brilliant analysis for the utterly confused throngs, save the day for LSU!

I always gave the Board more credit than that. Contrary to Wharton's and Roberts' portrayal, these were good, intelligent people, for the most part, who were capable of rendering knowledgeable judgments without constant interference by the Administration. Even Dr. Martin Woodin, then President of the LSU System, was represented to me as someone who would not assert himself. I would discover on my own how incorrect this depiction was. Woodin, who would become one of my closest contacts and friends on the LSU campus, was a great asset to the university, far more valuable than the lot of backstabbing politicians with which the main campus teemed.

Shortly before the date of the Board meeting, I was told by Roberts that if my recommendation to fire Stovall was approved, and there was no reason to believe that it wouldn't be, I would be asked to name a successor immediately. I got on the phone to Miami and finalized the deal with Arnsparger.

I also called Dolphin Head Coach Don Shula and explained my situation. He told me he would be sorry to lose Bill, but that he was happy his coaching companion of so many years was getting the break that no one would give him because of his age, which would be fifty-seven in a matter of weeks.

Wharton was very concerned that Arnsparger was an unknown. I assured him that anyone who knew anything about football, and that included the vast majority of Tiger fans, would not only know of Arnsparger's reputation for possessing one of the game's most brilliant minds, but would be amazed that LSU could lure him from the NFL.

The Good Old Boy Club, no doubt, had heard of Arnsparger, but its members weren't happy that he was about to become LSU's next football coach. For the first time in thirty years, the Athletic Director would have his man as coach, and that meant the perks would dry up.

The moment finally arrived, and on December 2, 1983, I entered the LSU Systems Building, Roberts on one side, my trusty bodyguard on the other. The room was packed with members of the media and as many members of the general public as the room would hold.

Big John McKeithen, former governor of Louisiana and prominent member of the Board of Supervisors, had already stated his intention to battle my recommendation to fire Stovall. He thought the Coach had the right to finish out the "one little old year left" on his contract. That was, he had reasoned, the honorable way all things in this state were done.

I found my seat in this foreign land and could almost see where the lines had been drawn. I suddenly realized that I was scared to death. I felt like little Dorothy who had dared to come before the Wizard to ask for a new brain for the strawman football program.

I gave a short synopsis of the season as it related to the future of the LSU football program and concluded with my recommendation that, for the good of LSU and the Athletic Department, Jerry Stovall be relieved of his duties as Head Football Coach of the LSU Tigers.

I had barely uttered my final syllable when McKeithen, the Wizard, began to bellow, and I stood at the podium, in respectful silence, for the duration of his forty-eight-minute rampage. Huey Long would have been proud of Big John's filibuster. He certainly didn't disappoint any of the room's 200-plus occupants who had come looking for fire-works.

He admonished me that firing Stovall could easily cost LSU tax dollars in the Louisiana Legislature at appropriation time. I wonder if he also feared that firing Stovall would cause a drop in the price of a barrel of oil?

He warned me that firing Stovall could drive a wedge between the university and its alumni, resulting in the cessation of donations and support to the school.

He cautioned me that Warren Rabb, an ex-LSU quarterback standing wild-eyed at the back of the room, wanted to beat me up.

Then, out of the clear blue sky, John McKeithen asked me, "Are you wearing a bulletproof vest?" Obviously, he wasn't aware of the police protection my family and I had been under for the past week and a half. Otherwise, he surely wouldn't have uttered perhaps the most stupid statement ever made in a public forum.

The former governor and I have since become good friends, and I have developed a great admiration and respect for this consummate politician, but he could easily have cost me my life with that ill-timed, ill-phrased remark.

The three-hour, thirty-minute public hanging concluded with a vote of 13-5 to accept my recommendation to fire Jerry Stovall. In the same breath, the Board voted 17-0, with Charles Cusimano abstaining, to empower me to negotiate a contract with Bill Arnsparger to replace him.

Amidst conflict, controversy and the character assassination of one Bob Brodhead, a new era in LSU football history began.

Jerry Stovall has since accepted a position with Louisiana National Bank. I am truly happy for him. Stovall was, and is, a good, kind man. But as a football coach, he had been projected into a profession that is demanding, at best. To those unprepared to handle it, it's also brutally unforgiving.

I sincerely wish that Stovall had been a good football coach. He was a promoter's dream: personable, well-spoken, popular. And he was an LSU hero.

But he came up short against the only measuring stick that counts in coaching, the won-loss column. Stovall's four-year coaching record at LSU stands at 22-21-3.

I have no regrets about firing him, because it was for the good of the program and the good of the university.

I wish Jerry well in the new life he and his wife Judy

have found, a life which is, he told me recently, a very happy one.

CHAPTER FOUR

What a Tangled Web
We Weave

LSU's twenty-sixth and newest Head Football Coach, Bill Arnsparger, was known as "The Defensive Genius" of the National Football League. Miami Dolphin Head Coach Don Shula, whose association with Arnsparger spanned one college and two NFL teams and close to twenty years, said his assistant possessed a "dedication, love and knowledge of the game of football which will help the Tiger program reap many, many dividends."

A.J. Duhe, former LSU defensive star who played for Arnsparger in Miami, called him "the best defensive coach in the country right now, at the college or pro level," and credited him with developing "more ideas and concepts about playing defense than any coach I've known."

I had watched Arnsparger in action for many years from my vantage point within the NFL, eventually as part of the same Miami organization, and I shared these sentiments. I was always most impressed with Arnsparger's ability to adjust to anything an opponent might throw his way.

Arnsparger had enjoyed considerable success as an assistant coach, particularly in Miami, where he built the famed No-Name Defense of the '70s and the Killer Bs unit that led the 1982 Dolphins to the Super Bowl.

His prior college coaching career spanned fourteen years and included stays at Miami of Ohio (1950), Ohio State (1951-53), Kentucky (1954-61) and Tulane University (1962-63). While on the Kentucky staff, Arnsparger established a close relationship with fellow assistant coach Don Shula, whom he would join in Baltimore, where Shula was Head Coach of the NFL's Colts. When Shula was named Head Coach of the Miami Dolphins in 1970, he took Arnsparger with him.

Following the 1973 season, Arnsparger was offered the head coaching job, his first, of the New York Giants. Two-and-a-half seasons later, he was fired, and Shula welcomed him back to Miami. Under Arnsparger's guidance, the Giants were 7-28.

My standard response to anyone who quizzed me regarding this tarnish on his otherwise impressive resume was to fault the Giants organization, saying that Arnsparger hadn't been given enough time to build a winner. It's a good thing my friend Wellington Mara, the Giants' owner, didn't read the Louisiana papers, or he would have grown tired of assuming responsibility for Arnsparger's low winning percentage. Perhaps he would have understood that I wasn't about to let the second guessers stand in the way of a smooth transition from the old coaching regime to the new.

Besides, ten years had passed since then, and Arnsparger's record of accomplishments spoke for itself. Nine times in his eleven full seasons with Miami, the Dolphin defense ranked either first or second in the NFL in scoring defense.

I was proud of my selection, and I was confident that Arnsparger would provide the leadership necessary to turn the football program around. I had better be. The Good Old Boy Club at LSU, smarting from its first setback in decades — and at the hands of an outsider, no less — was busy tying my fate to Arnsparger's future won-loss record. Either he won, or I lost.

Some members of the media were also less than receptive to the new coach. Ron Higgins, a local sports columnist, had written the following bit of prose in anticipation that Arnsparger would be hired: "Brodhead, who once had a job promoting nails, would have an easier time selling thumb tacks than Arnsparger.

"The four problems with Arnsparger in a nutshell? He's too old (almost 57 years old), he's from Miami (fans will point to Brodhead's so-called 'Miami Connection'), he's from the pros (LSU folks don't take kindly to a pro coach stepping into a college atmosphere) and he's not a proven major college winning head coach.

"If Brodhead wants to survive this ugly storm, he might consider shopping elsewhere for a head coach. Like at a major college."

Obviously, there wasn't going to be a run on red carpets to welcome Arnsparger, who was remaining with the Dolphins through the end of their season. I knew I had to do something. So I called my friends at ABC and asked for a favor. The Dolphins were appearing on a Monday Night Football broadcast the week after Arnsparger's appointment, and a few good words from Frank Gifford and "Dandy" Don Meredith would do wonders for my public relations campaign.

Not only were a few good words uttered from the booth, but praises were sung everytime Arnsparger appeared on camera, complete with frequent mention of the LSU program he would take over at the end of the Dolphins' season. Lo and behold, the skeptics in Tiger Town were singing a different tune in no time.

The same favor was granted again during the Dolphins' playoff telecasts, and by the time Arnsparger arrived on campus in January, I had created a living legend. The biggest problem I would face from that point on was that not only had the public bought the hype, so had Arnsparger.

Looking back, I remember hearing countless comments regarding Arnsparger's coaching abilities. I cannot, however, recall a single remark made on behalf of Arnsparger, the person. Allow me to fill the void.

In my dealings with Bill Arnsparger, I found him to be a shallow man with an unfriendly personality. His interests were few; in fact, if a topic didn't appear between the front and back covers of his playbook, he didn't want to talk about it. He'd rather transcribe it into the notebook he carried for recording all events as he interpreted them, which may or may not be as they actually occurred.

He was a poor public speaker who didn't try to hide the disdain he felt for anyone who might question his coaching expertise. I would spend a considerable amount of time, as would his wife, B.J., attempting to repair the burnt bridges he left in his wake. B.J. would prove better at it than I was. But she had more practice.

Arnsparger also had a deep-seated contempt for authority. Perhaps the years he spent watching Shula and Dolphin owner Joe Robbie at each other's throats rubbed off cn him, because from his opening press conference, when he proclaimed to the world that he was at LSU because he wanted to be (without so much as a hint that he might also be here because I hired him), to his final press conference three years later when, in announcing his resignation, he thanked people who hadn't known he existed prior to December 2, 1983, and didn't mention my name, Arnsparger's lack of respect for me and my position was always in evidence.

As the 1984 season approached, however, I had not yet come to the majority of these conclusions. At this point, I chalked up Arnsparger's unfriendliness to his preoccupation with getting the team ready for the season opener. He and B.J. bought a home just down the street from ours, and B.J. and Kay became inseparable friends. You never saw one without the other.

The 1984 season began on a sunny September afternoon in Gainesville, Fla., against the University of Florida Gators. My public relations campaign on the Coach's behalf was a rousing success, and a large contingent of the Tiger faithful had made the trip to witness Arnsparger's coaching debut.

As "The National Athem" played and I watched

Arnsparger stand, hat over heart, at attention with his team, I experienced one of my life's most emotional moments. I was so happy for him and B.J., who stood at my side with Kay in the visiting Athletic Director's box, I was moved to tears.

I was nearly as elated with the way Arnsparger's charges performed, coming back from a 14-0 first quarter deficit to tie the favored Gators, 21-21. Perhaps that's why I chose to ignore Arnsparger's contemptible displays at the game's conclusion towards two of his players.

Juan Betanzos had kicked a 35-yard field goal in the second quarter and a 43-yarder in the third to pull LSU to within one. His third attempt, made as time expired, was no good. When he approached his coach on the sidelines as the gun fired, he didn't get a comforting hug. He got brushed aside.

In the locker room afterwards, nose guard Roland Barbay was receiving fluids intravenously to combat the effects of severe dehydration. Arnsparger ordered the team bus to leave for the airport without him. I held the team's charter plane on the ground, or Arnsparger would have left Barbay and the team doctors with him to get back to Baton Rouge as best they could. Bo Strange, former LSU football standout and one of the doctors attending Barbay, would never shake the ill feeling caused by the incident, and after Arnsparger jumped him in the Alabama locker room the following season over the status of an injured player, Strange resigned.

The Tigers went on to win their next five games and climbed into the Top Ten of both wire service polls. Then Notre Dame came to town and knocked LSU from the ranks of the unbeaten with a 30-22 upset.

Following victories against Ole Miss and Alabama, the Tigers fell to Mississippi State, 16-14, in the final SEC game of the season. It appeared the Tigers, at 4-1-1 in conference play, had lost any chance at a Sugar Bowl invitation.

LSU closed out the season with a 33-15 victory over Tulane to finish Arnsparger's first season at 8-2-1.

But it wasn't over yet. The week after the Tigers'

regular season ended, Auburn blew its shot at the conference championship by losing to underdog Alabama. And thanks to an SEC decision to ban Florida, owner of the conference's best mark at 5-0-1, from any bowl appearances pending an NCAA hearing, LSU was Sugar Bowl bound for the first time since 1968.

Kay and I watched the Alabama-Auburn game on television, cheering like mad for the Tide. Seconds after Alabama did, in fact, upset Auburn, B.J. rushed through the door, and the three of us hugged and giggled and jumped up and down like little kids. B.J. had run from their house to ours in her socks.

Those were certainly the best of times for the Brodheads and the Arnspargers. After every game during the 1984 season, Bill and B.J. would stop in on their way home, sometimes as late as 1 a.m., and we'd raise a toast to the Tigers' successes. As they'd get up to go, Bill would shake my hand and thank me for giving him the opportunity to coach at LSU.

My daughter Mindy, knowing of Arnsparger's sweet tooth, baked him cookies before each game. He called them his "win cookies."

The Tigers Sugar Bowl opponent would once again be the Nebraska Cornhuskers, who had twice been ranked No. 1 in the nation during the 1984 season. Despite an outstanding first half of play, the Tigers would come up short against the Big Eight Conference co-champions. The final score was 28-10. The final AP poll of the season would rank LSU as the fifteenth best team in the nation.

Shortly after the Sugar Bowl, I noticed that Arnsparger was becoming increasingly independent and standoffish. During recruiting season, it was like pulling teeth to find out where he stood with the youngsters he was pursuing. Arnsparger was apparently afraid to keep me posted as to the success or failure of his recruiting efforts, lest he be subjected once again to the "he's too old to recruit" charges which had surfaced when he was hired. I guess he had forgotten that I was the one who had defended him against such criticisms in the first place. Or maybe he thought I had found out how heavily he had been relying on booster help to augment his visits to the kids' homes. Each recruit he was particularly interested in would meet with a local supporter at some point during his campus visit to discuss the possibility of summer employment.

Before I offered Arnsparger the job, I negotiated a contract with WJBO-AM for the broadcast rights to the LSU Head Coach's radio and television shows. I wanted to know how much WJBO was willing to offer before I entered into contract negotiations with any candidates for the job.

WJBO agreed to a two-year pact which would pay the next coach $120,000 a year, in monthly installments of $10,000 each. Using these figures, I negotiated Arnsparger's contract, offering him a base salary of $80,000 and a minimum guarantee of $80,000 in additional income.

It's a good thing I had hired Arnsparger for his coaching, not broadcasting, talents. His shows were artistic and financial flops. His personality came through loud and clear, unfortunately, and the programs were proving to be a tough sell. According to several people involved in the production process, Arnsparger was extremely difficult to work with, and his lack of consideration was a constant source of irritation.

By the time the broadcast contract expired two years later, WJBO had seen enough. Management notified me, and Arnsparger, as well, that in the future, they would carry only the radio portion of the deal. I had been privy to the financial statements for his TV program, and I didn't blame WJBO for wanting to cut their losses to the bone. Any chance of me intervening with WJBO on Arnsparger's behalf was effectively eliminated by Arnsparger himself, who had been making some very cutting remarks to the media about the much-publicized "bugging incident" in which I had been involved and which I will discuss, in length, in a later chapter.

When Arnsparger learned that his TV show had been canned, he made a desperate attempt to negotiate another package on his own. But his negotiating skills, like his on-the-air talents, left something to be desired, and he was finding it tough sledding. To this day, he doesn't know that I went behind the scenes and asked a local producer to take the show.

The new version of the Bill Arnsparger show fared no better, however, given the added burden of a little Florida trip the Coach undertook shortly before the start of the 1986 football season. But we'll get to that shortly.

According to several "listening posts" around town, Arnsparger deeply resented the fact that I had left him to negotiate his own television contract. He and B.J. were quick to bend any sympathetic ear with tales of my "terrible treatment."

I wish he had treated me as badly as I'd treated him.

At the SEC's annual spring meeting, I was subjected to yet another example of Arnsparger's insubordination when he staged a little scene at dinner one evening. He engaged me in a discussion, which soon dissolved into an argument, of a proposal which I happened to sponsor. He ended up calling it "ridiculous." I was highly irritated by his impertinence, particularly since the proposal involved a topic on which I was well-versed. I felt sure he had never run across it in one of his playbooks.

By this time, my administrative staff was beginning to show signs of revolution under Arnsparger's bullying tactics. The open hostility between several of my staff members and the Coach caused me a great deal of concern for several reasons. One, it was not conducive to productivity; two, I was very worried that it, like anything else in my office which hinted at conflict, might slip through the cracks to the media.

Arnsparger's treatment of the local media embarrassed me, and it horrified the Sports Information Department. During his Tuesday press conferences, Arnsparger would belittle any member of the media who asked him a question which was not to his liking; the media, in turn, would vent its collective frustrations on the Sports Information Department. It's a wonder the whole SID staff didn't call in sick every Tuesday morning.

I could never understand how the same media which took me to task on everything I said would bow to Arnsparger's dictatorial edicts, handed down weekly from the throne. The power of a winning football coach must truly be omnipotent, judging by those who came to kneel at the shrine each Tuesday.

I was relieved when spring arrived, and I concentrated on the success stories being written by the track, baseball, golf and tennis programs. The women's track team won the SEC indoor championship and would finish the season as the third-ranked team in the nation; the baseball team, which was attracting fan support for the first time in years, was ranked in the Top Twenty; the men's tennis team was ranked in the Top Ten; and the men's golf team, which had finished sixth in the NCAA tournament in 1984, was well on its way to another Top Ten finish.

The Athletic Department was finally on its way, and I revelled in these triumphs, oblivious to the storm clouds collecting on the horizon.

The summer months were relatively quiet on the LSU sports scene, and during the summer of '85, Kay and I were looking forward to a two-week cruise of the Mediterranean. The Arnspargers had made plans to take the same trip, and I had high hopes of reestablishing, at the minimum, a working relationship with the Coach.

The high seas didn't improve Arnsparger's disposition, however, and each attempt I made at shop talk met with the same reaction: nothing. I finally gave up and concentrated on the camels in Egypt. They were friendlier.

If isolation was what he wanted, isolation was what he would get. Apparently, Arnsparger didn't need my friendship. He had already taken the quickest path to autonomy, the one which circumvents the established chain of command. That's particularly easy to accomplish at LSU when one is a winning football coach and one's boss' boss is a frustrated-jock Chancellor.

Knowing the university faculty was down on the Athletic Department for its "football factory" reputation, Arnsparger sought to endear himself to the academic community and thus solidify his relationship with Wharton.

With the help of a retired Army colonel, Arnsparger painted a very believable picture of concern for the scholarly pursuits of his athletes. I had hired the colonel in question, Larry Fitzmorris, the year before, on the advice of Charlie Roberts. Fitzmorris, former commandant of the LSU ROTC Corps, was to run the Academic Counseling Department. Once Arnsparger arrived, however, Fitzmorris took to calling himself the Head Coach of Academics and began spending more time at football practice each afternoon than he did tending to the academic needs of LSU's 200 non-football-playing athletes.

The Arnsparger/Fitzmorris duo launched a campaign which implied that the other head coaches, particularly Head Basketball Coach Dale Brown, didn't have to "play by the rules." It charged that while the football players were made to toe the academic line, the other athletes were allowed to miss class and skip study hall. Funny, I saw no mention in this campaign of the correspondence courses entered on behalf of football players and the work which was being completed by proctors and tutors who reported to Fitzmorris and were paid with Athletic Department money.

I was later to find out that Fitzmorris had knowledge of a particularly disturbing problem involving a sociology course.

The course in question was being recommended by Academic Counseling to an unusually high number of athletes, particularly those in apparent grade trouble. I never thought anything of the course until word reached me that several athletes who had taken it during the 1986 spring semester had been caught cheating.

Within hours, Women's Basketball Coach Sue Gunter was in my office. One of her players had been accused of cheating. I also learned that a member of the football team, as well as the daughter of an Athletic Department employee, were involved.

When I heard the rumor that a great many athletes might be implicated, I jumped into the problem. I sent for, and received, a list of athletes taking the course over the past two semesters. The number topped fifty. In addition, the list revealed that a large number of the athletes taking the course received As or Bs.

With a little more investigating, I soon had in my hand a handwritten copy of the exam. I questioned the athlete who had given it to me, and he told me that the exam had been provided to him by the course's professor. It appeared to me that I had just discovered the reason for the abundance of high grades.

I asked for an appointment with Carolyn Hargrave, Vice Chancellor of Academic Affairs and Provost of the university. She told me that Fitzmorris and Dean Greg Blimling had been investigating the matter for several days.

I headed for Blimling's office, where I was told that the investigation had turned up three casualties: one football player, one basketball player and one nice kid. All three, I was told, would probably be suspended from school.

In the end, they were. The professor, on the other hand, was simply told that he could no longer teach the course involved.

I was appalled that I had been left out of an investigation of facts pertaining to our athletes. I was equally disturbed that Fitzmorris, who, along with Arnsparger, had portrayed me as someone who condoned a double standard when it came to academics, chose not to notify me of the situation.

It was during the fall of 1985 when the bugging incident I referred to earlier occurred. While the full explanation of that event is still to come, allow me to mention it here as it pertains to Arnsparger's treatment of me.

Rather than offering his support through my ordeal,

Arnsparger offered his other cheek. When the media would question the Coach about the situation, he would answer that he, his staff and his squad had remained "above" such distractions and that he did not care to discuss it. With each "no comment" he uttered, Arnsparger hammered another nail into my coffin.

That fall also saw Dale Brown invite *Sports Illustrated* to town in yet another of his quests for publicity. Brown hoped the trip would result in a feature about his never-ending, uphill battle against society, in general, the NCAA, in particular. But once *SI* writers Curry Kirkpatrick and Gary Smith hit campus, they couldn't resist the drama and intrigue of the bugging story, and it became the secondary focus of their stay. "Hello, Trouble, I'm Dale Brown," the ten-page cover story, would be preceded by the six-page "Isn't This Unbelievable?" account of everything from the "vanishing" of freshman basketball player Tito Horford to my plight.

Kirkpatrick told then-Sports Information Director Joe Yates and me that during the course of his research for the story, he had talked to a number of people who said they wished they could take the credit for "setting me up." Given that, he also told us that the thrust of the story would be the effects of the bugging incident on the university, not the "setup" itself. It seems an athletic director being caught in a sting wouldn't make for good reading. Maybe the real story never does.

The "Crazy Days at LSU" edition of *Sports Illustrated* hit the newsstands on November 18, 1985. Within hours, Brown and I were up to our eyebrows in the wrath of the academic community. In addition, I received ultimatums from several Board members to get rid of Brown. I refused. I was in the process of negotiating a new contract for him.

Arnsparger seized upon the *SI* stories as the excuse he would need in the event he came up short in his recruiting efforts prior to the 1986 season. "Of course, Bob's problems and Dale's problems . . . it's all been really negative,"

Arnsparger was quoted as saying in the local afternoon paper: "I'm sure that type of publicity doesn't help you."

Despite being asked about such things "in probably every home he visited," Arnsparger signed nineteen recruits to national letters of intent, including what columnist George Morris called "perhaps the best prep running backs in Texas, Florida and Louisiana." Even Arnsparger had to admit that, "I kept reading where we were catching up. I guess we caught up."

Arnsparger also credited "non-athletic sources," including Fitzmorris, Wharton and members of the faculty, with much of his recruiting success.

The 1985 football season, which saw the Tigers finish with a 9-1-1 record, proved to be a roller coaster ride over the wire service polls, and on "pick-um" day, when the bowls issued their official invitations, LSU was ranked seventeenth. Tennessee would finish 5-1 in conference play to the Tigers' 4-1-1 to earn the Sugar Bowl bid, and, given LSU's less-than-impressive ranking at the time, the other New Year's Day bowls weren't interested.

The best deal available was being made by Liberty Bowl Executive Director Bud Dudley, who was willing to take a chance on the seventeenth-ranked team in the nation. The Tigers finished the season with victories over Notre Dame, Tulane and East Carolina, and Dudley's gamble paid off. The final poll of the season ranked LSU twelfth, and the Liberty Bowl got an attractive matchup between the Tigers and the Baylor Bears for its December 27 classic in Memphis.

While Baylor was a respectable club with an 8-3 record and a stingy defense, I was confident it was a club that LSU would handle with ease. A victory here would not only move the Tigers into the Top Ten in the season's final polls, it would give LSU its first ten-victory season since 1961. The stage was set for a dramatic ending to the year.

In Baton Rouge, preparation for the trip to Memphis was well under way when Arnsparger decided to assert his new claim on independence and assume responsibility for the team's travel plans. While this was a drastic departure from the standard operating procedure which saw all such arrangements handled, always competently, by my Business Department, a full-fledged argument with Arnsparger would only serve to create more controversy. Since that was something I could do without, I reluctantly gave in to his demands.

Arnsparger insisted that the players be given travel money and allowed to drive their own cars to Memphis. Can you imagine ninety football players, ranging in age from eighteen to twenty-two, who live for five months of the year with every second of every day planned for them, suddenly having cash, freedom and wheels in Memphis for the holidays? Neither could Memphis, and the Liberty Bowl staff told me afterwards that the team absolutely terrorized the city for one solid week.

On the field, the quality of play certainly reflected the good times had by all. Baylor embarrassed the Tigers for four quarters, and when the gun mercifully sounded, the final score was 21-7.

B.J. embarrassed us in the Liberty Bowl's VIP Box, where we had ill-advisedly been placed with officials from Baylor. The Baylor group was understandably voicing their pleasure over their team's performance, much to the displeasure of Mrs. Arnsparger. At one point, she said some very offensive things to one of the cheering Baylor fans. Unfortunately, the fan was the president of the university.

I was mortified and slipped out the door and down the hall to the coaches' box. I should have stayed where I was. This performance was even more embarrassing than the first one I had witnessed. Having called a few plays myself over the years, I knew that what I had walked in on was the most disorganized and confused attempt at game calling I'd ever seen.

Obviously, Arnsparger's preoccupation with pre-game administrative duties had come with a steep price tag.

Hindsight being 20/20, I should have stepped in and demanded that the team be transported by charter plane, as originally planned. At the time, however, I was tired of my increasingly frequent run-ins with the Coach and had sought the course of least resistance.

One Sunday morning the following month, my phone rang at 7 a.m. It was Arnsparger, asking if he could come see me. Assuming he wanted to discuss recruiting or another of his favorite topics, such as the lack of football tickets available to him, I told him to come ahead.

He entered my house without so much as his usual fishy handshake. He had come to talk, he announced, about the *Sports Illustrated* article on Dale Brown. He demanded that I do something about the situation immediately. If I refused to act, he said, he was going to Tampa Bay to interview for the defensive coordinator's job with the NFL's Buccaneers.

My response to his threat was simple: "Go ahead. I found one of you, I can find another."

That, apparently, was not what he wanted to hear, and off he went to inform the Chancellor of his plans.

I wasn't worried. I had learned a long time ago that coaches and power plays go hand in hand. You just waited until they played their cards, then you bluffed right along with them. From the looks of it, this power play wasn't going to be any different than the others I had seen, even if the player was a "defensive genius."

I didn't believe for a minute that Arnsparger would walk away from the adulation bestowed upon him as the head coach of a successful major college football program. At least not to become just another assistant coach on just another mediocre NFL team. But I also knew that the Chancellor wouldn't share my confidence. I was sure he wouldn't be able to stand up under the pressure of Arnsparger's ploy.

I called several of my closest associates and summoned them to my home for a strategy meeting. We determined that the best approach was to alert the Chancellor to what was coming and warn him not to fall for it.

By the time I arrived at the Chancellor's house, Arnsparger had come and gone. I could smell the deceit the minute I walked through the door.

I sat down. It's a good thing I did.

Wharton began his speech by telling me that the university could not afford to lose Bill Arnsparger and that I should get down on my hands and knees and beg him to stay. He ended it, several sickening minutes later, by telling me that Arnsparger was more important to the university than I was.

I couldn't believe what I was hearing. Arnsparger wasn't responsible for the Athletic Department's financial and competitive successes. I was. I told the Chancellor that there were plenty of Bill Arnspargers out there for the taking, and that I didn't think it was wise for a university administrator to hitch his wagon to a football coach. What I thought obviously didn't matter. The wagon hitching had long since taken place.

I don't know if Arnsparger went to Tampa Bay for an interview or not. I assume that he did, although the issue never surfaced again. I also assume that Arnsparger and the Chancellor cut some sort of a deal that morning and that the athletic directorship came up during the course of the discussion.

I now found myself an outsider, forced to watch the football recruiting process from afar. During this time, the Arnspargers gave a party at their home for the top recruits and their parents and invited the Chancellor and his wife, as well as several members of the coaching staff. The Brodheads did not receive an invitation.

In fact, I may not have found out about the party at all had not a catering bill, which had been submitted directly to the Chancellor for approval, been accidentally rerouted to me by someone in his office. Seems that not everyone was in on the game of "ring around the chain of command" being played. I put the invoice in my desk drawer and waited to see how long it would take before someone started to squirm.

I didn't have to wait long. B.J. soon came looking for her money. She wasn't known for her patience in financial matters. In fact, if the monthly $10,000 check her husband received for his broadcasting endeavors was a day late being cut, she'd call WJBO to inquire as to its whereabouts. One of her dun calls would often send a radio station employee scurrying, check in hand, for her mailbox.

Encouraged by the Chancellor and Roberts, Arnsparger began travelling exclusively in administrative circles. Following a pre-season speaking engagement in Shreveport attended by several members of my staff as well as the Chancellor's, Arnsparger flew home on the Alumni Federation's plane rather than on the one which carried the Athletic Department representatives. In fact, I don't remember him saying a word to me all evening.

I saw what was happening, and I couldn't do anything to stop it. The bugging ordeal left me too wounded to fight.

For two years, I had devoted a great deal of time and energy to an ambitious plan to improve athletic facilities at LSU. I will detail the project in a later chapter; here, suffice it to say that it centered around a privately financed expansion of Tiger Stadium, which included a state-of-the-art athletic dormitory/administrative complex.

Arnsparger, I would discover, was opposed to my project and told several people that he thought it was foolish to spend a lot of money on facilities for sports other than football. He later told the Chancellor in my presence that he did not relish the pressure which would be brought to bear upon football to "foot the bill" for a high-priced complex for sports that nobody in Louisiana cared about.

In the end, the project was shelved, thanks, in part, to the subversive efforts of Arnsparger and Wharton. Sadly, they had succeeded in wrecking, for selfish reasons, the very vehicle by which the LSU Athletic Department would have gained national acclaim.

As the 1986 football season approached, the battle

lines appeared drawn. And when I left for Chicago on August 18 to attend a "Special Meeting of Athletic Directors," the time to launch the attack had arrived.

I had been looking forward to the meeting, which had been called by Georgia Tech Athletic Director Homer Rice, with great anticipation. Facing an attempt by the university Presidents' Commission to gain control of college sports, the athletic directors of the nation's major colleges were being brought together to devise a plan to halt the mounting takeover.

I arrived in Chicago the evening before the meeting was to begin, and I joined a group of my SEC counterparts for dinner. I sat with Bill Carr of the University of Florida, who had resigned his position a few months earlier but had agreed to stay on until a replacement could be found. We discussed his plans for the future, and I wished him well. Carr is a bright, dynamic man and an absolute credit to the profession. I told him I would would miss his input at our annual conference meetings.

After dinner, we returned to the hotel, and I turned in. I wanted to be well rested for the next morning's session.

The first series of meetings proved most interesting, and by the time the Chair announced the lunch break, we had touched upon a variety of topics. We adjourned for the morning, and I remained behind to talk with Frank Broyles, Athletic Director of the University of Arkansas, about future scheduling.

I had noticed when Carr left his chair a few minutes earlier, and as the room emptied, he returned, visibly flustered. He approached me and told me that he needed to speak with me. Now. And in private.

Once we were alone, Carr began to apologize to me. For what, I didn't know, and I stood there, dumbfounded. Then he explained.

He had left the room, he told me, to call his office and check in. Someone there had given him the message that Bill Arnsparger was flying into Gainesville that night to be interviewed for the Athletic Director's job.

I was shocked. Arnsparger had not requested my permission to be interviewed by another university. He was supposed to be in Baton Rouge getting a football team ready for the season opener, two weeks away.

Carr swore to me that he was as shocked as I was and that Arnsparger's name hadn't even been on the list of interviewees when he left Gainesville the day before.

I was embarrassed as the word spread throughout the delegation. A reporter from *USA Today* stopped me in the lobby and asked me if I had a comment about Arnsparger being interviewed for the Florida job. I did, but I kept it to myself and headed for my room and the telephone.

My secretary told me that Arnsparger had waited until I left for Chicago, then requested a meeting with Wharton, LSU System President Allen Copping and, from what I could gather, several members of the Board of Supervisors. Once the meeting convened, Arnsparger presented those in attendance with a list of grievances against me and my administrative style. One of his assistant coaches later told me that during the compilation of his list, Arnsparger had asked his staff to provide him with any complaints they, too, may have had.

Arnsparger's list was as lengthy as it was phony, and it was just one part of his power play.

Part two was to ask permission of Wharton to interview for the Florida job, which Wharton granted without waiting for me to return and respond to Arnsparger's charges.

Nine hundred miles away in Chicago, I spent the rest of the afternoon on the telephone, sifting through the pieces, lining up support from my allies on the Board and trying, in vain, to get a call through to Wharton or Copping.

I called Defensive Coordinator Mike Archer and asked him to hold the staff together. I needed him to inject calm into what I imagined must be a desperate situation developing in Baton Rouge: a leaderless staff, a confused squad, an AWOL head coach and Game One just two weeks away.

I also phoned several other assistant coaches and told

them their jobs were secure.

I had a lot of thinking to do on my late-evening flight home. I didn't know what awaited me in Baton Rouge, but I knew the next few days weren't going to be easy.

When I awoke the next morning, my mind was made up. The damage Arnsparger had done was, in my opinion, irreparable. I wanted his contract terminated and him sent to Florida, neatly packaged. And I wanted Archer named interim Head Coach.

Before leaving for Gainesville, Arnsparger told his team that Florida officials had contacted him about the Athletic Director's job and that he was making the trip "just to talk about it."

I believed he was making the trip to stir up controversy in the Athletic Department. And I deeply resented it.

The coaches I spoke with assured me that Arnsparger's absence was causing no problems in the football office, and that the "desperate situation" I had imagined from Chicago was, in fact, just that. Imagined. Preparation for the season opener was continuing without a hitch. In fact, I got the distinct impression they didn't care if Arnsparger returned from Florida or not.

On the practice field, the players began to tease each other with the sound that reverberates through Florida's stadium on game days. It sounds like the theme song from the movie *Jaws*. To me, it sounded like the team had figured its coach had become a Gator.

On the announcement board in the locker room, a message appeared.

"Where's Bill?" it read.

"Who Cares?" someone had scrawled beneath it.

My sentiments, exactly.

The day after I returned from Chicago, Wharton summoned me to his home to present me with Arnsparger's grievance list. After I read it, Wharton reminded me that Arnsparger was far more important to the university than I was. He also warned me that I would not survive Arnsparger's departure and suggested, once again, that I beg him to stay.

Had the bugging incident of months before not put me in such a precarious position, I would have blown Arnsparger away with what I knew about several questionable recruiting efforts, among other things. Instead, I was forced to meet once a week with the Chancellor and Arnsparger to review the grievance list and assess the progress I was making towards amending my ways.

I would also be forced to take part in two phony press conferences, which saw me at one end of the table and Arnsparger at the other, vowing that there was no rift between us, while the Chancellor promised to do his best to maintain the peace if only Arnsparger would promise to stay.

Arnsparger announced that he was withdrawing his name from the list of candidates for the Florida Athletic Director's job. He, in fact, did no such thing and later accepted that position.

As I got up to leave the Chancellor's house, he asked me a most interesting question. Did I think Arnsparger would double-cross us?

The guy's been had and doesn't even know it, I thought to myself.

"In a New York second," I said to the Chancellor and walked out the door.

Arnsparger's grievance list, diplomatically entitled "Problems to be Resolved," follows, exactly as I received it from Wharton. I have added my reaction to each entry.

"PROBLEMS TO BE RESOLVED"

"I. Academics — Objective: Consistent handling of all academic matters to ensure athletes meet their responsibilities and all are given proper assistance.

"Solution: Transfer Academic Counseling for Athletes to Vice-

Chancellor for Academic Affairs."

My reaction: Arnsparger, with the help of Fitzmorris, had portrayed himself as the only member of the Athletic Department who was concerned with the education of the athlete.

I was concerned enough that I spent a year, along with one of my assistants, Mike Mallet, in developing and implementing a new curriculum entitled "Non-Teaching Coaching and Sports Administration." I was disturbed by the large numbers of athletes majoring in General Studies, and I felt that the courses offered under the new program would not only offer them meaningful training, but would enhance their chances of securing employment after graduation. Apparently that didn't qualify as "proper assistance" in Arnsparger's book.

"II. Student Life — Objective: Safe, clean dormitory.

"Solution: Continue renovation of Broussard Hall to include carpets for all areas. Funds for part of carpeting will come from private sector. Security system will be added to Broussard Hall and persons will be on night duty. Policies regarding use of Broussard Hall will be developed."

My reaction: While Arnsparger had busied himself with finding carpet donations for Broussard Hall, I had worked for two years to develop the plans for a multimillion-dollar athletic complex to house all LSU athletes. I had even participated in a study to develop color schemes and furniture designs most conducive to productive dormitory study time.

Athletes would have lived on the fourth, fifth and sixth floors of the state-of-the-art complex, and the only access to the dormitory area would have been provided by security-coded elevators.

Arnsparger had raised "funds for part of carpeting" in the private sector. (The rest, I was to learn, would come out of Athletic Department earnings.) My project was also to have been funded through the private sector, but I had devised a way to raise *all* the money I needed, which, by the way, was a bit more than the amount Arnsparger required, about $27 million more.

As to the "policies regarding use of Broussard Hall," they had been developed long before I arrived at LSU. How did Arnsparger justify including them in a list of grievances against me?

"III. Renovation of Football Office and Other Facilities supporting football program.
A. Football Office
B. Squad Meeting Room
C. Area for Graduate Assistants
D. Weight Room
E. Training Room

"Solution: Discussions will take place involving Chancellor, Athletic Director and Head Football Coach to determine extent of renovations required for effective support of the program. Work will begin as soon as associated plans can be developed. Funding from concessions auxiliary."

My reaction: Under this entry, Wharton's heavy-handed editing becomes apparent, since the commitment of funds ("from concessions auxiliary") far exceeded the scope of Arnsparger's authority. By sanctioning Arnsparger's proposed renovations of the football office and facilities, Wharton, in my opinion, appears to have broken five state and/or university policies or procedures:

1. The Board of Supervisors had approved the plans for my project on several occasions. Ignoring the Board's endorsement in favor of Arnsparger's proposals, which had not been submitted for approval, was contrary to university policy.

2. Commitment to a renovation project without state capital outlay approval violates state policy. Even if funding was to be provided by an Athletic Department auxiliary, the request for appropriation of such monies must be submitted to the Appropriations Committee of the State Board of Regents.

3. Work on a state project does not begin "as soon as associated plans can be developed." Final approval must first be sought from several state and university entities.

4. Committing Athletic Department funds without first seeking the approval of the Board is against university policy. So is committing profits from a self fund-generating auxiliary of a department without the approval of the head of that department.

5. Any commitment made to renovating the football office or facilities without the knowledge of the Athletic Director or the Board of Supervisors violated the university policy which states that decisions affecting a department should be made with respect to the established chain of command.

"IV. Ticket policy of the Board of Supervisors in support of football program will be followed:
   A. Recruiting
   B. Jobbers
   C. Courtesy Cars: Coaches will be provided adequate transportation for recruiting.
   D. Assistant Coaches
   E. Players
   F. Head Coach
   G. Etc.

"Solution: Discussions will take place to determine if revisions in the current policy are required."

My reaction: Tickets were a sore point between Arnsparger and me from the onset of our relationship. He was never satisfied that the number he was allotted was sufficient.

I would learn, however, that the coaching staff had more than enough tickets. A number of football supporters informed me that they could purchase extra jobber or recruiting tickets as late as game day from Recruiting Coordinator Sam Nader.

I cannot respond to the ticket needs expressed in items (D), (E) and (F) because I have no idea what the problems were.

The only control I had over courtesy cars was to be sure they were provided in adequate numbers, which they were.

Maybe Arnsparger's last item, (G) Etc., contained the real problems under this grievance entry. Everything that comes before it was a lot of hot air.

"V. Per Athletic Director's job description — Head Coach of Football will be given input into determining the football schedule. Head Coach and players will be given input into bowl game selection."

My reaction: The fans and alumni of LSU have long lived with the belief that a great football tradition exists here. In reality, the Tigers hadn't won a national championship since 1958.

There had been a great many winning football teams at LSU, but an inordinate number of those victories had come at the expense of sub-500 opponents.

I am a firm believer that one builds a great football program by playing the best teams in the nation. So I replaced Rice, the University of Richmond and William &. Mary with a ten-year pact with Texas A&M and a home-and-home deal with Ohio State.

Arnsparger, who didn't share my scheduling philosophies, complained to me on several occasions that there weren't enough weak teams on the schedule.

Arnsparger's proclamation that the "Head Coach and players will be given input into bowl game selection" evoked a simple response from me: No they wouldn't. As Director of Athletics, it was up to me to make the decisions which would prove most advantageous to the Athletic Department as a whole. That did not include placing a million-dollar decision into the hands of a football coach, or subjecting it to the whims of a group of twenty-year-old football players. That went out when the 1959 squad voted not to go to the Sugar Bowl.

"VI. Drug Program — Discussions to determine best overall program. Team physicians, coaches, students and athletic staff. Procedures to be established to ensure integrity and effectiveness."

My reaction: Arnsparger chose to attack the existing Athletic Department drug program, which my staff and I had worked very hard to develop and which was, in my opinion, a most comprehensive approach to a very serious problem, because he wanted to exclude me from any knowledge of or involvement in drug-related matters. I would later find out that Arnsparger's idea of the "best overall program" was the one which allowed him to deal with cases of detected abuse according to the "value" of the athletes in question. In print, his stated desire was to "ensure integrity and effectiveness" with his established procedures. In practice, he apparently wanted to ensure something else: "eligibility."

"VII. Travel — Adequate Travel for:
  A. Recruiting
  B. High School Clinics
  C. AFCA Clinic
  D. SEC Rules Clinic
  E. Visit other Schools' Spring Practice

F. Pro — Camps
G. Alumni
H. Tigers Unlimited
I. Civic Clubs
J. Etc."

My reaction: Why "Travel" even found its way onto a list of grievances against me is a mystery. Not only had Arnsparger and his staff never wanted for travel funds, they were often reimbursed by the group requesting their presence.

Perhaps the Coach found it necessary to make "Travel" a complaint against me because I had put a stop to his practice of flying in chartered airplanes, a practice which, by mid-1986, had cost the Athletic Department in excess of $50,000.

"VIII. Equipment
A. Film and Projectors
B. Video Tape and Equipment
C. Word Processor
D. Phone System — LD Service"

My Reaction: Since the Athletic Department had plenty of film and projectors and video tape equipment, and since "LD Service" smacks of insignificance, I must assume that the real problem here was (C) Word Processor. The Athletic Department had one of those, too, but Arnsparger wanted his own.

In private, the Chancellor agreed with my assessment that a second word processor was unnecessary; in meetings with Arnsparger and me, however, he never put his foot down.

"IX. All Areas of Decision
A. FB Staff
B. Rec. Coordinator
C. Administrative Assistant (New Position)
D. Trainers (2) and Student Assistants (Decisions for

salary increases, etc.)

E. Equipment Mgr. (1) and Assistant & Student Assistants

F. Strength Coach (1), Assistant and Student Assistant — under A.D.

G. Maintenance of stadium & practice field."

My reaction: Arnsparger enjoyed total input in (A) through (F), making recommendations to me in areas of salaries, increases and hirings. I would gladly have given him responsibility for "(G) Maintenance of stadium & practice field," but his resume failed to mention that he had prior experience in the area of groundskeeping.

"X. Sports Info. — Media Guide. Rec. Coordinator (new), Recruiting Brochure and other recruiting aids (schedules, calendars, posters) or public relations."

My reaction: Winning records, bowl games and national television appearances attract athletes to a football program, not glossy pictures and catchy phrases. I nixed Arnsparger's request for a recruiting brochure because I believed it represented an unnecessary expense.

I wonder what Wharton's colleagues on the Presidents' Commission, with their "cutting costs on unreasonable expenditures" approach to intercollegiate athletics, would have thought of his endorsement of this capital outlay. Perhaps "cutting costs" doesn't apply when chancellors and head coaches are cutting deals.

"XI. Area, or room for entertaining recruits, parents, on game day and on recruit weekends. Did use L-Club before 1985; now use corridor in Assembly Center, and it's OK if nothing else available. Needs dressing up. Parking for visitors (Reddoch)."

My reaction: Once again, my athletic complex would have

provided for such needs. I assume this grievance was included to give Arnsparger a place to say the present accommodations were "OK" and deny the necessity for any elaborate new structure.

CHAPTER FIVE

A Question of Ethics

Within the Louisiana Department of Civil Service, there is a Commission on Ethics for Public Employees, domiciled in Baton Rouge. According to the Code of Governmental Ethics, "the commission shall consist of five members to be appointed by the governor, with advice and consent of the Senate, who shall appoint one member representing organized labor, one member representing business or industry, one member representing agriculture, one member representing recognized professions, and one member with a demonstrated interest in civil service employees." These people are charged with administering and enforcing the Code of Governmental Ethics and the "regulations, rules and orders issued hereunder with respect to public employees."

There also exists a Board of Ethics for Elected Officials, which is charged with administering the same code with respect to elected officials.

While the ethics bodies are made up of different people, both share the same office as well as the same executive secretary.

In its Declaration of Policy, the Code of Ethics proclaims: "It is essential to the proper operation of democratic government that elected officials and public employees be independent and impartial; that governmental decisions and policy be made in the proper channels of the governmental structure; that public office and employment not be used for private gain other than the remuneration provided by law; and that there be public confidence in the integrity of government. The attainment of one or more of these ends is impaired when a conflict exists between the private interests of an elected official or a public employee and his duties as such. The public interest, therefore, requires that the law protect against such conflicts of interest and that it establish appropriate ethical standards with respect to the conduct of elected officials and public employees without creating unnecessary barriers to public service . . ."

As I interpret this verbiage, the Ethics Code was enacted to protect the general public from those who would use their office or position to gain financially at the expense of those he was elected or appointed to serve, and the ethical standards set forth by the code to protect the public interest must not interfere with the fulfillment of the subscribed duties of the official or employee.

The Commission on Ethics for Public Employees would play a central role in my stormy tenure at LSU. In fact, I would earn the dubious distinction of being the most frequently cited public employee in Louisiana history.

Time after time, I was summoned to appear before the commission to defend myself against charges that I had violated the Code of Governmental Ethics. Time after time, in determining that I had, indeed, committed violations, the commission would conclude that either I had no prior knowledge that the action in question would constitute a violation or that I had realized no personal benefit or gain through such action. Yet on October 8, 1986, Chancellor Wharton cited possible code violations committed by me to bring about the beginning of the end of my LSU career. His official statement read:

"I have received the report from the State Commission on Ethics for Public Employees alleging that LSU Athletic

Director Bob Brodhead has been involved in improprieties that may constitute violations of the Louisiana Code of Governmental Ethics. In view of these allegations and other recent events, I have suspended Mr. Brodhead with pay."

What follows is a running account of my four-year relationship with the Ethics Commission. Some of the events below resulted in an investigation and subsequent dismissal by the commission; the rest were deemed violations of the Code of Governmental Ethics.

During the summer of 1982, my first on campus, I hired a young television genius from Philadelphia, Pa., Tom Ficara, and charged him with developing and implementing a regional pay-per-view television network to carry all LSU sports.

I had known Ficara for a number of years and knew he was eminently qualified for the task. Before his thirtieth birthday, Ficara had conceptualized an "all day, all sports" programming format, compiled a library of sports video tapes to meet the programming demands and formed a corporation to act as a supplier to cable stations. Undercapitalized, the corporation eventually failed, but his programming concept was a sound one. In fact, it was the formula eventually adopted by ESPN and made successful on a national level.

Under Ficara's guidance, "Tigervision," as we named it, was to enjoy considerable success and become one of the most innovative applications of the electronic media to athletics in the history of college sports.

Tigervision was a contractual agreement between LSU and Total CATV, a large, sophisticated cable company located in Baton Rouge. It represented a major undertaking by CATV, which would be responsible for absorbing all costs, including production equipment and studio setups. It also represented an opportunity to make a good deal of money, and revenues would be shared equally by LSU and CATV after expenses were met.

Before Tigervision kicked off with the 1982 football season, Ficara and I were to recommend a broadcast team, which CATV would carry on its payroll. After considerable thought, we decided that Paul Hornung and Jim Taylor would work as well together in the broadcast booth as they once had in the Green Bay Packer backfield. We also decided that to appeal to the large number of LSU fans who were women, we should add a feminine touch to the telecasts, and we set out to find a female sideline reporter.

When our search proved unsuccessful, Ficara suggested we try my daughter, Mindy, who had attended her first football game at age three to watch her dad quarterback the Cleveland Bulldogs of the old United Football League past the Wheeling Ironmen. Thanks to my involvement in pro football for most of her life, Mindy's knowledge of the game certainly qualified her for the job. If that didn't, the fact that she had graduated *cum laude* from Wake Forest University in communications did.

We arranged for an interview with CATV management, and Mindy was hired for the modest sum of $75 per game. She did a good job, and both CATV and the Athletic Department received a great many positive phone calls about her performance.

At the conclusion of the football season, Mindy was asked to handle the color commentary for women's volleyball and basketball. She agreed and was to be paid $50 per game for her services.

Before the winter sports season hit the halfway mark, the Ethics Commission, acting upon the complaint of a local sportswriter, undertook an investigation of her CATV employment, and she and I, along with CATV President Dr. Tony Currier, were summoned to appear before its members.

After our testimony, the commission found that Mindy's continued broadcasting work would constitute a violation of the Ethics Code on the grounds that I had control of the contract with CATV. This ruling was handed down despite my testimony that I had absolutely nothing to do with the day-to-day operations of CATV and that the contract

between the cable company and LSU had been signed, sealed and delivered before Mindy was offered the job.
To avoid further charges, Mindy quit.

During the summer of 1984, I made a concerted effort to sell to an advertiser the blank spaces beside each of the two count-down clocks in Tiger Stadium. These four-foot square spaces, which had never been utilized, were extremely marketable because of their visibility: Where is the first place a fan looks when the team stays too long in the huddle or on the line of scrimmage? The advertising message which appeared beside the twenty-five-second clocks would enjoy a great deal of exposure.

I convinced Sheldon Beychok, a member of the Board of Supervisors and owner of Sunbeam Bakery, from which every food-serving entity of the university bought its bread, of the marketing value of this space, and sold it to him for $6,500 for the year.

Some time later, the Ethics Commission issued several advisory opinions that this transaction could not be completed on the grounds that Beychok, as a member of the Board of Supervisors, could not enter into a contract with the university. These opinions were also applied to the bread contract between LSU and Beychok's Wolf Baking Company, Inc.

Eventually, the First Circuit would render a decision that members of the LSU Board of Supervisors and their companies may enter into contracts with the university if the contract is awarded by the lowest sealed competitive bid. In a letter to University President Allen Copping regarding the First Circuit decision, University Attorney Shelby McKenzie wrote: ". . . we do not find any language in the decision which questions" the university's right "to enter into negotiated contracts for sale of advertising rights."

At the time of the Ethics Commission's determination, however, the sale of the space in question was prohibited, and the Chancellor ordered me to cover the painted message, already in place, with black vinyl.

Also during the summer of 1984, a group of LSU fans and boosters gave a testimonial dinner for me at a restaurant in New Roads, La. This supportive group of people not only wanted to express their appreciation to me for a job being well done, they also were familiar with the need for discretionary money in the Athletic Department to cover those things (entertainment, country club or social club dues, etc.) which are an integral part of a "people business" such as college athletics.

Having a discretionary fund, for which the money has been raised in the private sector, does not violate state or university policies. Using discretionary monies to cover entertainment-related expenses incurred by an athletic department is allowable by the NCAA.

Tickets for the testimonial dinner were $200 apiece, and there were approximately 120 people in attendance. I was told that a number of those people had come as guests of ticket holders, and that approximately $15,000 had been collected. After the restaurant bill was paid from the gross proceeds, the remainder went to pay a few small entertainment-related bills.

Once again, however, the Ethics Commission received an official complaint, and an investigation was commenced.

As the inquiry would eventually prove, I had nothing to do with the planning of the event. Nor did I receive the exorbitant amount of cash reported by *Tiger Rag*. Additionally, a testimonial dinner given to raise money, in the private sector, for a discretionary fund did not violate the Ethics Code. And yet I was subjected to speculation in the media as the result of another Ethics Commission investigation.

To this day, no one has explained to me how my dinner differed from the hundreds of such events held annually in Louisiana on behalf of politicians to raise hundreds of thousands of dollars for their campaign funds. For that matter, no one has explained to me how an Athletic Department discretionary fund differed from the one which still exists in the LSU Foundation on which the Chancellor periodically draws for entertainment-related purposes. Like the Athletic Department fund, the Foundation fund contains money raised in the private sector. Unlike the Athletic Department's fund, it has managed to escape the scrutiny of the Ethics Commission.

During 1984, I undertook to replace the track in Bernie Moore Stadium, the facility named after the great football and track coach of the 1930s and '40s, which looked like it was of the same vintage. Joggers and any variety of weekend athlete had been allowed to use the facility without restriction, and the track had suffered considerable damage as a result. The running surface was dangerous to the track team members using it, and it was an embarrassment to the university.

My assistant in charge of facilities, Bill McClure, a name well known in the world of track and field, had advised me that the state-of-the-art running surfaces were to be found in Germany, and before we made our final decision regarding the type of track to be installed, we should see them in person.

To finance such a trip, we turned to Tigers Unlimited, the non-profit corporation which had been formed to raise funds for athletic scholarships and improvements to Athletic Department facilities. Tigers Unlimited, a registered, private 501 C3 corporation, would also be building the track facility in question using donations from the private sector, so it seemed the logical place to look for travel money.

In the meantime, McClure and Assistant Track Coach Sam Seemes were invited to Germany by Spurtan, a manufacturer of running surfaces, to view as many tracks as possible before determining which one would best suit LSU's needs. At the same time, McClure and Head Track Coach Billy Maxwell were invited to fly to Sewanee, Tenn., at the expense of another track manufacturer, American Servicing, to inspect a facility at the University of the South.

The Tennessee trip was completed in a day. The trip to Germany, paid for by Spurtan, lasted four days, during which time the twosome inspected and evaluated more than twenty track facilities. In fact, the trip produced the plans for the original design of the track facility completed at LSU during the spring of 1987. It also realized a savings of more than $4,000 in travel expenses.

The proposed facility was put out on bid and awarded, according to university policy, to the lowest bidder, which was neither Spurtan nor American Servicing. Months later, the Ethics Commission received a complaint regarding the paid-for trips, and another investigation was launched.

This one concluded that I had violated Section 1117 of the code by authorizing my employees to receive a "thing of economic value" from a potential vendor, despite the finding, issued in the same opinion, that "because of the number of facilities visited, particularly on the trip to Germany, these employees had no opportunity to do anything during these trips except visit tracks. In other words, these trips were of no personal benefit or value to the respondents."

In addition, the commission concluded that "Mr. McClure and Coaches Maxwell and Seemes violated Sections 1111 A and 1115 A of the code by having received a 'thing of economic value' in the form of travel and related accommodations" from the two track manufacturers in question.

It was with great interest that I read a recent account in the local newspaper detailing the acceptance of campaign contributions by the Mayor of Baton Rouge from persons and companies who later received hundreds of thousands of dollars in "preferential business" from the city. I did not, however, read of any pending investigation by the Ethics Commission's Board of Ethics for Elected Officials.

Perhaps the "thing of economic value" rule doesn't apply to elected officials from Louisiana, just public employees from Miami.

On April 18, 1986, the bugging incident, which will be

detailed later, came to a judiciary head. Rather than close the book on the matter, however, the court ruling merely set the stage for a second, albeit less impartial, determination of my fate.

On Monday, April 21, the Athletic Council met to discuss the ruling and formulate the recommendations it would make to the Board of Supervisors on April 25, the date of its next regularly scheduled meeting. The Athletic Council and its role in the aftermath of the bugging incident will be detailed in a later chapter. For now, however, allow me to briefly state that I was prepared to fight the sanctions it had authored, and my plans were making Wharton and University President Allen Copping very nervous. As a result, they requested that I not attend the Friday Board meeting and recommended that I go ahead with the vacation plans I had cancelled when I learned of the Athletic Council's proposals.

The vacation in question was the annual trek Kay and I made to LaPaz, Mexico, located on the Baja Peninsula, as guests of Douglas Manship, publisher of Baton Rouge's two newspapers and owner of several radio and TV stations here and across the country. Manship frequently entertained friends at a private club to which he belongs in LaPaz, and Kay and I had been treated to two previous vacations at this plush resort overlooking the Pacific.

Before the Athletic Council revealed its plans for me, I was looking forward with great anticipation to getting away from the pressures of the past several months and spending time with my good friend. After the council meeting, I called Manship and told him, regretfully, that the importance of my appearance before the Board had just usurped my need for a vacation.

When the top two administrative officials of the LSU System told me to go ahead with my plans, however, that's exactly what I did. I called Kay to tell her the Baja was on again and that we'd fly out of Baton Rouge on Friday morning.

Before we left town, a reporter from New Orleans called and asked if I planned to be at the Board meeting. No, I told him, I was going to the Baja with Doug Manship for a few days' rest. I didn't think twice about revealing my plans, particularly since the trip bore the seal of approval of the Chancellor and President of the university.

The story of my trip appeared in the New Orleans newspaper, and it wasn't long before the Ethics Commission received a complaint. This one, I was told, was signed by *Tiger Rag* part-timer and Louisiana Network Sports Director Jim Engster.

Louisiana Network is a rival of Southern States Network, which holds the exclusive radio rights to broadcast all LSU athletic events. The complaint alleged that because a Manship-directed company, Baton Rouge Broadcasting, owned Southern State's flagship station, WJBO, my trip gave Southern States an "unfair advantage" over its competitors. How this alleged "unfair advantage" was to have occurred is unclear to me, since the contract between Baton Rouge Broadcasting Company and LSU had been entered into on December 22, 1982, three years and three months prior to the trip in question and fifteen months prior to my first Baja vacation with Manship.

In fact, when the radio deal was signed, I had yet to meet Manship.

Nevertheless, the commission would determine that ". . . Mr. Brodhead violated Section 1115 A(1) of the Code by accepting as a gift the round-trip air transportation to Baja, Mexico, and the associated lodging and other accommodations, under circumstances such that the gift was given to him by Mr. Manship at a time when he, Mr. Manship, was both an officer and director of a person, Baton Rouge Broadcasting Company, Inc., which, in turn, had a contractual relationship with LSU."

The commission also found that Manship had violated Section 1117 of the code "by giving Mr. Brodhead something which he, Mr. Brodhead, was prohibited by virtue of the application of Section 1115 A(1) of the Code from receiving."

Shortly after Manship and I were charged with violations of the Ethics Code, the following article appeared in the Baton Rouge newspaper:

"LAWMAKERS WARNED
NOT TO ACCEPT FREE TRIPS"
"A state ethics board Tuesday warned legislators not to go on hunting trips paid for by lobbyists, but said it would take no action against lawmakers who may have already done so.

"In a four-page opinion, the Board of Ethics for Elected Officials said it has evidence that some legislators accepted air fare, lodging and related accommodations in connection with a dove-hunting trip sponsored by an oil company whose lobbyists work with the legislature.

"Such trips violate the state Ethics code, the opinion said.

"The Board's staff attorney refused to say who the lawmakers were, when or why they took the trip.

"In the opinion, the Board said, 'The ends of justice nevertheless would be best served if the board declined to conduct public hearings to receive evidence and to determine whether or not particular violations of the code within its jurisdiction may have occurred.

" 'The purpose of the opinion is to admonish elected officials in general and members of the legislature in particular that the board views the Code of Governmental Ethics as prohibiting elected officials from accepting as a gift travel, lodging, food and entertainment from those persons registered as Louisiana lobbyists as well as persons who engage for compensation the services of lobbyists,' the opinion said."

Why did the Board of Ethics for Elected Officials

decide that it would "take no action" against the legislators who had accepted a dove hunting trip from lobbyists, while the Commission on Ethics for Public Employees decided to charge me with a violation of the Ethics Code for accepting a fishing trip from a friend with whom I had no direct business dealings? Why did the board's staff attorney "refuse to say who the lawmakers were," while the commission released my name to the public? Why would "the ends of justice be best served" by sparing the legislators "public hearings . . . to determine whether or not particular violations . . . may have occurred," while I was made to appear before the commission and defend myself, in just such a public hearing, against charges that my trip may have been a violation of the code?

In its October 29, 1986, editorial on the issue, the local morning newspaper said: ". . . it doesn't take a mental giant to see the inconsistency, unfairness and blatant political considerations which guided both these rulings . . ."

Allow me to pose yet another round of questions: If, in fact, Manship owns the radio station from which the university receives more than $400,000 annually in cash and game programs by virtue of the broadcast agreement, how was the university able to accept a multimillion-dollar contribution from Manship to the School of Journalism, when I could not accept a fishing trip of significantly lesser value? Why was it alleged that Manship took me on a fishing trip to influence the radio contract when the same allegation was not applied to Manship's very large gift to the university? Someone of lesser scruples than Manship may very well have viewed the donation as a way to secure the extremely valuable broadcast rights to LSU athletics. Is that any more preposterous than assuming he took me fishing as a means to the same end?

As disturbing as the Ethics Commission's finding was, I remain equally distressed by several attendant issues. Foremost is that my immediate supervisor, Chancellor Wharton, not only knew of each of the three vacations I had taken with Manship, he, along with President Copping, had encouraged me to take the trip which was investigated by the Commission. Before I left on trip number two, he had asked me to intercede with Manship on his behalf. Wharton had, on several occasions, expressed to me his belief that Manship did not like him, and he thought that a few good words from me might prove beneficial to him and/or the university.

The Ethics Commission failed to consider Wharton's knowledge of — and consent to — my trips with Manship. This is the same commission that had concluded, in its opinion dated February 27, 1986, that "Respondent Brodhead violated Section 1117 of the code by having authorized Mr. McClure and Coaches Maxwell and Seemes to receive a 'thing of value . . .'" in the form of paid-for trips to Germany and Tennessee. The same commission that found McClure, Maxwell and Seemes guilty of violating Sections 1111 A and 1115 A of the code "by having received a 'thing of economic value' " failed to consider that the invitation Manship extended to Kay and me during the spring of 1985 was also extended to, and accepted by, Bill and B.J. Arnsparger.

In retrospect, I wonder if the "thing of economic value" rule would apply to several hunting trips taken by Wharton and Charlie Roberts?

On two occasions, Sam Friedman, a member of the Board of Supervisors, invited Wharton, Roberts and me on white-wing dove hunting trips to Mexico at his expense. Wharton and Roberts accepted both invitations. I was forced to decline the invitations because both times, something came up at the last minute which prevented me from going.

These trips may, in fact, violate Section 1115 A of the code because Wharton and Roberts, as public servants, were prohibited from accepting a thing of economic value from a person with whom LSU had a "contractual or other business or financial relationship." Friedman qualified as such a person by virtue of the fact that he was an owner of a Holiday Inn located outside of Gainesville, Fla., the hotel at which the football team stayed when it travelled to Gainesville to play the University of Florida.

While the Ethics Commission was investigating my vacation, it stumbled upon "The Bob Brodhead Show," my weekly call-in/sports-talk radio broadcast which had aired, at that point, for two-and-a-half years. The program was broadcast each Monday night from 7 to 8 p.m. on, you guessed it, WJBO.

"The Bob Brodhead Show" placed a particular emphasis on discussions of the "minor sports," those non-revenue stepchildren to which no one had paid much attention until I arrived on the scene. I viewed my radio show as an excellent device by which to promote the Athletic Department, in general, and the non-revenue sports, in particular.

During my first year as Athletic Director, my radio program was broadcast by WWL out of New Orleans. A New Orleans advertising firm handled the sale of advertising for the show, bought the time on WWL and, after it paid its sales commissions, split the net between John Ferguson, the show's host, and me. After the show's first two months, however, the net was not. In fact, the only time I saw any money at all was early in the project's history, when I received a grand total of $1,100.

The show was becoming very popular, however, and a growing number of listeners were tuning in to hear me promote LSU athletics, so I continued to make the 150-mile round trip each Monday night without compensation. By the end of the school year, I had finally grown weary of the long drive, and when George Jenne, WJBO station manager, approached me about a weekly, Baton Rouge-based radio show for the following year, I enthusiastically agreed.

My arrangement with WJBO was very simple. I would assist the station in contacting potential advertisers for the program, and if enough advertising time was sold prior to the beginning of the broadcast season in late August or early September, the show would go on the air. In return, I would receive $300 per show.

Prior to the 1985-86 school year, I asked Mark Jeffers, an assistant in the Athletic Department's Promotions Department, to help me contact potential advertisers. I didn't find my request to be anything out of the ordinary; for years, Ferguson, in his capacity as Director of Development at LSU, had sold ads for Jerry Stovall's show. Jeffers managed to sell just three ads, and that was the last time I asked for his help in this endeavor.

During the course of the Ethics Commission's preliminary inquiry into my radio show, Jeffers told the investigators that I had forced him to resign because he had announced his refusal to sell ads for the following year's broadcasts. I had, in fact, asked Jeffers to resign, but my reason had nothing to do with this alleged "refusal." In the first place, I had not or would not ask Jeffers, based on his lack of success during the summer of 1985, to sell ads for next year's show. I asked him to resign because I had been handed information which indicated that Jeffers may have been leaking confidential and sensitive Athletic Department matters to people outside the department. I will detail my discovery in a later chapter.

Jeffers apparently repeated this fabrication to the Chancellor, who, despite having knowledge of the information I had in hand and despite the University Personnel Department's concurrence with my recommendation that Jeffers be asked to resign, offered the young man another position within the university system.

At the conclusion of its investigation, the Ethics Commission determined that my radio show constituted a violation of Section 1111 C(2)(d) because I had received "a thing of economic value in the form of the monetary payments for each of the several 'Bob Brodhead Shows' from an entity, Baton Rouge Broadcasting Company, Inc., which, in turn, was prohibited by reason of Section 1115 A(1) of the Code from giving Mr. Brodhead a gift. As Baton Rouge Broadcasting Company, Inc. was prohibited by Section 1115 A(1) of the Code from giving Mr. Brodhead a gift, then Mr. Brodhead was therefore prohibited from receiving any thing of economic value for services rendered to that entity."

The commission also found that Baton Rouge Broadcasting had violated Section 1117 of the Code "by having provided Mr. Brodhead with a thing of economic value which he was prohibited from receiving by reason of the application of Section 1111 C(2)(d) of the code."

In its infinite wisdom, the commission failed to consider that virtually every football and basketball coach in the state of Louisiana has a radio program, and that they are paid handsomely for their services. At LSU, Arnsparger received $40,000 a year for his radio show, and Basketball Coach Dale Brown received $20,000 for his.

Outside the realm of athletics, Dr. Loren Scott, head of the LSU Economics Department, hosts a monthly television program on WBRZ-TV, which also happens to be owned by Manship. Why is it not a violation of the Ethics Code for this department head to have a television program on a station owned by a person who has "contractual or other business or financial relationships with the public servant's agency"?

The commission also concluded that my continued receipt of $300 per week for "The Bob Brodhead Show" would constitute a violation by Baton Rouge Broadcasting Company and me of "controlling sections of the code." Therefore, "this relationship must cease and . . . Mr. Brodhead must discontinue rendering the service for which he is being paid by the Baton Rouge Broadcasting Company, Inc."

The commission did allow that neither Manship nor I was aware that my being compensated for the radio show constituted a violation of the code. Ignorance is apparently no defense in the eyes of the commission, however, as evidenced by the following: ". . . public servants and persons in general — and Mr. Brodhead in particular — are charged with knowledge of the State's conflicts of interest statute and violations of these sections of the code do not require actual knowledge that the questioned conduct is, indeed, prohibited."

If "Mr. Brodhead in particular" is charged with knowledge of Louisiana's conflicts of interest statute, couldn't

Chancellor Wharton, who falls under the heading of "public servants and persons in general," also be charged with such knowledge? Wouldn't Wharton's knowledge of my radio show constitute a violation of the conflicts of interest statute?

Wharton not only knew that I had a radio show (how does one hide a radio show, after all?), he occasionally listened to it, judging by his Tuesday morning comments to me regarding call-ins I had received the night before. And not only did Wharton occasionally listen to the program, he allowed two departments of the university, Alumni Affairs and Continuing Education, to advertise on it.

Was the Chancellor charged by the Ethics Commission with violating the Ethics Code because he had knowledge of my radio show? Were the Chancellor and President charged with violating the code because they encouraged me to accept Manship's invitation to the Baja rather than appear at the April 25 meeting of the Board?

And justice for all?

SACKED!

CHAPTER SIX

A Formidable Opponent

Sheldon D. Beychok is a burly, imposing figure who has managed to frighten most of the LSU academic community with his tyrannical outbursts of temper. Many times, Chancellor Jim Wharton expressed to me his fear of this powerful member of the Board of Supervisors, and I've heard countless stories told of Beychok's volatile disposition and sharp tongue.

I would find out for myself how dangerous an adversary Beychok could be.

Beychok's power base is not financial. His string of unsuccessful business ventures includes the ill-fated New Orleans Jazz of the National Basketball Association and the bankrupt Wolf Baking Company, Inc. Rather, his power base is purely political, with campaign headquarters located in the back room of Gus Piazza's Phil's Oyster Bar. There, Beychok holds court, and topics of debate range from LSU athletics to any number of institutional matters on which stances are assumed without the benefit of full Board discussion.

Piazza, one-time manager or All-American assistant trainer at LSU, caters these sessions. Had I known how important some would prove to my future at LSU, I might have frequented the establishment on occasion.

On May 21, 1982, I appeared before the Board of Supervisors to be interviewed for the job of Athletic Director. Charlie Roberts had spent hours beforehand coaching me on what to expect from each Board member. He filled me in on everything from their respective likes and dislikes in the area of athletics to how they were likely to react to certain answers or statements on my part. By the time the Board meeting arrived, I was thoroughly indoctrinated. I felt I knew each one of these strangers intimately.

Roberts had warned me that Beychok was a "snake in the grass" who was sure to "voice the minority's opinion" along with his colleague, Charles Cusimano of New Orleans. He told me that while I was to take what Cusimano said with a grain of salt, I should be alert to Beychok's questioning. If anyone could hurt my chances of being hired, Roberts said, it was Beychok.

During the interview, Beychok surprised me by remaining very quiet. When Wharton made his formal recommendation that I be named Athletic Director, the Board voted 13-1 to accept. Beychok had cast his vote for me. Cusimano, true to half of Roberts' prediction, had not.

Beychok and I actually began our relationship on very congenial terms. And we remained friends until the first time I dared say to him what few ever did: "No."

It didn't matter that the request Beychok made was not in what I considered to be the best interests of the Athletic Department. He did not take kindly to being refused, and I quickly saw that mentioning Cusimano and Beychok in the same breath was like trying to find similarities between a goldfish and a piranha.

My first run-in with Beychok came over my decision to assume control of the Athletic Department's concessions from the current concessionaire. As I've detailed earlier, my initial audit of this function uncovered numerous problems due to a lack of institutional control, and I had set out to convince the surprisingly reluctant Administration of the merit of my plan. I hired Pat O'Toole from the Orange Bowl to handle Athletic Department merchandising and help me assemble the necessary data.

Within a short period of time, we had accumulated sufficient evidence to make a formal presentation to the Board. Not much escapes O'Toole's practiced eye. He got his start in the business by selling hot dogs at the old Forbes Field in Pittsburgh, Pa., where his dad was concessions manager. While I was with the Miami Dolphins, I hired O'Toole from Cleveland Stadium to run the Dolphins' concessions at the Orange Bowl. In two short years, what had been a losing venture became a money-maker. O'Toole is known throughout the sports industry as the best in the business.

Regardless, Beychok was furious with my proposal to have the Athletic Department manage its own concessions. He vowed to fight it with such a vengeance that he aroused my suspicions.

The Ogden Corporation, a nationally known concessions management company which handled the Louisiana Superdome's merchandising and concessions operations, was Beychok's choice to become the new Athletic Department concessionaire. While Ogden enjoyed a good reputation in this cash-and-carry industry, it was nevertheless in the game to make money. I was of the belief that such money should be made by an in-house concessions operation, and that a middleman was unnecessary. I was also of the belief that internal concessions would provide the quality products and service that Tiger fans deserved.

Concessions companies follow an accepted practice of offering big up-front money and/or finders' fees to help secure long-term contracts with clients the size of LSU's Athletic Department. My figures showed that even up-front money wouldn't add up to what in-house concessions would generate, and I was determined to win the Board's approval.

Beychok, in the meantime, was attacking my plan from every angle. Internalized concessions would be too expensive to staff; it wouldn't make any money; it was a bad business deal. But his arguments ceased on the day of the Board meeting at which the issue would be decided. His threatened filibuster never materialized.

I would later learn that such behind-the-scenes maneuvering was standard operating procedure for Beychok. Time and time again, I would prepare for a battle at the Board level with Beychok. Time and time again, the battle never came to pass. Perhaps Beychok knew that I always did my homework when my majority backing from the Board was at stake, and the onus to prove me wrong would be on his shoulders.

My proposal that concessions be taken in-house received the Board's unanimous approval. To date, under O'Toole's watchful eye, the concessions operation has generated in excess of $2.5 million in profit for the university.

My second encounter with Beychok began with his determination that I needed a special consultant for the newly created Tigervision network and pay-per-view television. His recommended annual salary for such a position was a tidy $40,000. Beychok suggested that I talk with his friend, Fred Rosenthal.

Rosenthal, Beychok told me, had once worked in some capacity at the Baton Rouge Riverside Centroplex and possessed an extensive background in promoting arena events. I agreed to speak with the man and found him well-versed in these endeavors. I also found he had little or no experience in the new field of pay-per-view television, and I turned thumbs down on Beychok's request that I hire him.

The result of my action was that for an extended period of time, Beychok refused to entertain any proposal I might bring to the Board. Regardless of the issue, the arguments in its favor or its potential impact on the Athletic Department or university as a whole, Beychok simply and consistently voted "nay."

It was soon apparent that my trips before the Board would be facilitated by a good working relationship with Beychok. I needed to find a way to reestablish the friendship we had enjoyed initially. I stumbled upon just such an opportunity almost by accident.

After a grace period in which the Chancellor allowed me to run the Athletic Department without interference, he had begun to establish an ever-tightening grip on its operations. It was taking more and more of my time to prevent his meddling from adversely affecting the department's day-to-day functioning.

I needed to erect a barrier the Chancellor would respect, and I thought of Beychok. If ever there was a force which could get Wharton to back off, it was the fear of Beychok's wrath. In addition, Beychok might appreciate that I had turned to him for help and allow me back into his good graces.

I called Beychok and told him that I needed to see him. He agreed to a meeting and invited me to his office. I explained my dilemma with the Chancellor, and he seemed very sympathetic. At the meeting's end, he promised to help and told me that what we had discussed would remain between the two of us.

Not only did Beychok's promise of help go unfulfilled, but he also informed Wharton of our confidential meeting. Wharton, needless to say, was not pleased.

My next episode involving Beychok proved to be the most bizarre. It also proved just how deeply Beychok's animosity for me ran.

On a spring evening in 1984, my daughter Mindy and I were watching a wrestling match in the LSU Field House. The crowd was sparse, and anyone entering the building was easily noticed. Much to my surprise, the Chancellor walked through the door and approached the far end of the bleachers. Since I had never seen him at a sporting event other than a football or basketball game, I knew something must be wrong.

When he caught my eye, he motioned to me, and I walked to where he was standing. He was obviously upset about something, and he told me that Charlie Roberts was waiting for us in his office.

I walked back to where I had been seated and handed Mindy the keys to my car. "This might take a while," I told her. "I'll get a ride home."

At this point, allow me to provide some background information to this peculiar situation. As I've stated earlier, LSU's track facility was in deplorable condition, and I had initiated a project to replace the running surface. Word of my intentions was out, and the competition between various track manufacturers to land the job was heating up. I was being visited daily by a number of these firms' representatives, and some were beginning to submit proposals.

David Brantley, a young Baton Rouge businessman who owned and operated a sports surfaces installation company called No Fault, was among my visitors. Brantley had learned of the project in its infancy and had mounted an ambitious campaign to secure the bid.

At the conclusion of one of several meetings Brantley had initiated with my assistant Bill McClure and me, he told us that he "would do whatever it takes to get the job." Exchanging a quick look with McClure, I said to Brantley, "What it takes is being the low bidder on the track surface that my coaches want."

After Brantley left, McClure and I joked about his statement, wondering just what it meant. I remembered being told by a prominent group of Louisiana contractors that a certain percentage was always built into bids given on LSU projects to "take care of the jockey," and I wondered if this was what had been implied. I also remembered being told by this same group that many businesses steered clear of submitting such bids for that very reason.

As Wharton drove me to his office, I had no way of knowing that what I was about to learn was no joking matter.

Roberts, indeed, was waiting for us, and he had in his possession an audio tape which he claimed had been given to him by a local businessman.

The businessman, Roberts said, had somehow come across the tape, and after listening to it, had headed for campus to find me. When I couldn't be found, he had looked up Roberts, given him the tape and sworn him to secrecy. That's as much as Roberts said he knew about the tape's origins, although now, I'd take better-than-even odds that Roberts knew more than he was saying.

The tape, Roberts continued, had been made of a telephone conversation between two men, at least one of whom was talking on a car phone.

The Chancellor wanted me to hear the tape, and he put it into his tape player. The machine was badly worn, however, and it wouldn't play. After several unsuccessful attempts, he resorted to rigging it with a couple of pennies, and it finally worked. What I was about to hear was well worth the wait.

As the tape began, I thought back over the events of the preceding week, which were suddenly fitting together like pieces of a jigsaw puzzle. Gov. Edwin Edwards had called to tell me that David Brantley had asked him for a recommendation on the installation of the new track. Edwards did his duty and proclaimed to me the importance of doing business with a Louisiana-based company. In closing, however, the Governor earned my never-ending gratitude. "Bob," he said, "get the best deal for LSU. I know you will."

Over the years, as I've listened to the various accounts of the alleged transgressions attributed to the Governor, I remember the treatment he afforded me during my career at LSU. Perception isn't always grounded in fact; it's often painted by a thousand hostile brushes.

The second telephone call I received concerning the new track was from Beychok, who, in the most reconciliatory of terms, told me he was calling on behalf of a Baton Rouge-based track installer called No Fault Industries. Beychok said he didn't know the company's owner, David Brantley, but that he was a good friend of his older brother, Beaver.

As a Board member, Beychok continued, he was interested in seeing that LSU got the best track facility available. As a taxpaying citizen, he said, he felt that Louisiana's interests would be best served by doing business with a local company.

He concluded by saying that he wanted to be sure No Fault received the proper specifications for the job and an equal opportunity to be awarded the bid.

While I had never seen Beychok at a track meet (in fact, I'd never heard him express any interest in the sport), I thanked him for his call and assured him that No Fault would receive the same consideration as any other company involved in the bidding process.

As the tape rolled, it was immediately apparent that the two speakers had an intimate knowledge of the resurfacing project.

One of the voices described to his friend the request made of the Governor to call me. He said that "Shelly" was going to follow that call with one of his own, but that he was going to tell Brodhead that he didn't know David Brantley, he knew his brother.

The voices referred to me as that crazy Miami bastard and worse, and gleefully spoke of jamming it down my throat. There were several remarks made which implied that whatever they planned to jam down my throat would find its way out the other end, as well.

Then one of the voices mentioned "knee-capping" me, and I froze. From what I'd heard of this particular form of knee surgery, I wasn't interested.

The conversation continued with a discussion of a project at another state-supported university for which a specific resurfacing company had received the specifications "from the inside." It seems the bid had been written to that company's particular product, which had virtually assured the company of being the only bidder capable of filling the order.

I'd heard enough to conclude that the two speakers did not care for me a bit, and I was more than a little concerned for my safety. I wanted to either confront Beychok and clear this thing up before it went too far, or turn the matter over to the District Attorney. My well being had been threatened. In addition, the tape had detailed a possible conspiracy to defraud the taxpayers of Louisiana.

I asked the Chancellor what he planned to do about the situation. He told me he wasn't going to do anything until the university attorneys heard the tape and offered their opinions.

Within the next ten days, the tape was played for Shelby McKenzie, a university attorney, in the presence of the Chancellor and me. McKenzie echoed my sentiments that the tape was serious business and that something should be done. I was not privy to any ensuing conversations which detailed what that might be.

In fact, that was the last time I was to hear the tape. Sometime later, I was told that it had been handed over to the District Attorney and that the subject had been dropped.

Beychok and I would also butt heads over the selection of a strength coach for the football team. I had just hired Bill Arnsparger, who was in the process of building a coaching staff, when I learned that the Nicholls State strength coach was the Back Room's nominee to fill the same position at LSU.

Beychok made a strong pitch for the man, and I asked Arnsparger to grant him an interview. I also told him that the vacancy was his to fill.

Arnsparger agreed to talk to the man, but the chemistry wasn't right, and the coach rejected the candidate hands down. Beychok voiced his displeasure to anyone within earshot of Phil's Oyster Bar.

My final head-on confrontation with Beychok was the first to be conducted publicly. It centered around my Stadium Project, to which Beychok was opposed from the word go.

I made my initial presentation to the Board on January 25, 1985, and the project drew rave reviews. Not surprisingly, it drew a lone, but vehement, vote of dissent.

"I voted 'no' for a lot of reasons," Beychok was quoted

as saying by the January 26 Baton Rouge *Morning Advocate*. "Generally, it was a matter of the football tail wagging the academic dog again. This university is passing a golden opportunity for making money for the university. This new facility will not give one professor a pay increase. It will not take one graduate student who can't speak English out of the classroom . . .

"It will take a lot of energy and focus away from academic fund raising. We simply don't need it. Nobody can tell me why the little darlings (LSU's athletes) need a better place to sleep."

Apparently, Beychok hadn't kept up with the university's history of fund-raising failures, and he obviously had skimmed over my figures which projected a windfall for LSU academics. In fact, as I will detail in the next chapter, the Stadium Project would have raised more money for the university on an annual basis than any other individual source. The "athletic tail" would have wagged the "academic dog" to the tune of $600,000 a year!

Allow me to conclude this chapter with a final account of the role Beychok played in my tenure at LSU. During the spring of 1986, I received a telephone call from Roberts. I was surprised to hear from him, since we had long since ceased to communicate with any regularity. I was even more surprised by his stated purpose for calling.

He had just returned from a trip which Beychok and the newly appointed President of the LSU System, Allen Copping, had also taken. Roberts told me that on the plane ride back to Baton Rouge, he had pretended to be asleep, while in fact, he was listening to the conversation being held between Beychok and Copping.

The discussion, Roberts said, centered around an attempt to influence me to resign. Roberts also told me to be very careful during the next few days, because rumor had it that there was a move coming out of Phil's Oyster Bar to replace me as Athletic Director with former LSU basketball great and current Converse shoe company executive Joe Dean.

Within forty-eight hours, I was summoned to Copping's office. Wharton was already there. Copping began to lament the rocky road I had been forced to travel as LSU's Athletic Director, and he nearly broke into tears at the recollection of the trials and tribulations to which my family and I had been subjected. He told me he wouldn't blame me if I just said, "To hell with it," and bid LSU farewell.

"I appreciate your concern, Allen," I told him, "but I'm no quitter."

With that, I promptly added another name to the ever-growing list of people at LSU I knew I couldn't trust.

SACKED!

CHAPTER SEVEN

A Vision
for the Future

Repeated mention has been made throughout the preceding chapters of my Stadium Project and the controversy it engendered. Initially, I was amazed by the seemingly inexplicable opposition the plan encountered. Hindsight, however, has shed a great deal of light on its many detractors and their reasons for wanting it stopped. But I'm getting ahead of myself.

During the fall of 1984, I embarked upon an in-depth fact-finding mission which took me to the universities of Alabama, Georgia, Florida and Tennessee as well as to Auburn. The purpose of my journeys was to assess the facilities at the Southeastern Conference's athletic elite and determine where LSU stood in comparison.

What I learned was that while the actual physical layout at LSU was second to none of those I visited, our facilities were far behind others in the SEC. Each university I toured had magnificent athletic management facilities, dormitories, physical rehabilitation set-ups, dressing rooms and administrative offices either in place or on the drawing board. The programs with which LSU had to compete for the best high school athletes had been busy expanding and improving their physical plants, and LSU had been left behind.

Under construction at the University of Alabama were a two-story, 66,000-square-foot football facility and the Paul Bryant Museum, which would house a continuing education center, a 150-room hotel and an alumni office. The University of Florida had recently unveiled O'Connell Center, the $14-million, 12,000-seat indoor arena, and its football stadium had been upgraded in 1982 with the addition of twenty-eight "sky boxes." The University of Georgia had begun work on a four-level, $10-million athletic complex, and the University of Tennessee was in the process of building a 25,000-seat basketball arena.

When LSU's facilities were built, they were possibly among the finest in the nation. Sadly, they had been allowed to rest on their laurels. No one had figured out that a depreciation reserve should have been established to fund replacement and/or renovation efforts.

One of the first documents I was handed upon my arrival on campus in 1982 was an engineering report which did everything but condemn Tiger Stadium. The primary problem the report detailed was the erosion of concrete which, if left unchecked, would eventually affect the stadium's reinforcing steel, rendering the structure unsafe. In other words, it wouldn't be long before Tiger Stadium would fall down and go boom.

Also aging less than gracefully was Broussard Hall, LSU's athletic dormitory which had been built in the late 1950s. Many of its restrooms leaked, thanks to the antiquated plumbing system, and the decor had deteriorated to the point that it was best described as early American trash. In short, Broussard Hall was an absolute embarrassment.

When recruits were brought onto campus, every effort was made to cut a wide path around the athletic dormitory. Representatives of other schools readily admitted to me that Broussard Hall was one of their most effective recruiting tools. Mere mention of its dilapidated condition was often enough to deter a prospective LSU signee faced with living there for the next four or five years.

Even the Assembly Center, the 14,000-seat indoor arena which had been completed just twelve years earlier, had become filthy due to the lack of a maintenance program and, I might add, professional management. I had often watched as spectators tried to position themselves on the upholstered seats in such a way that their skin wouldn't touch the stained surfaces.

I was always surprised, during my travels across the state, by the number of times I heard about the wonderful facilities I had inherited. The truth of the matter was that the program I had been handed was so financially starved that even basic preventive maintenance chores had been deemed too costly. The funding for upkeep on these once-marvelous facilities simply wasn't there, and the neglect had taken its toll.

Recruiting gifted prep athletes is the name of the game in college athletics, and it's no longer enough to offer a youngster a scholarship. Call it window dressing. Call it marketing. Call it what you will. In today's high-stakes competition for the best young talent, you also have to offer him or her the opportunity to live and compete in the finest facilities. It was a matter of keeping up with the Joneses, and LSU wasn't.

Given the Athletic Department's demonstrated inability to raise private funds, I knew I would have to look elsewhere to remedy the situation. Given the financially strapped condition of the state's economy, turning to the taxpayers wasn't an alternative.

The more I looked at the situation, the more convinced I became that if I had to come up with the money to satisfy the most pressing of our needs, which was the prevention of further deterioration to Tiger Stadium, then why not come up with an all-encompassing wish list? Why not find a way to improve the entire LSU athletic complex at the same time?

I tore a page from professional football's success story and set out to introduce LSU's athletic facilities to the 21st century.

The NFL's most profitable revenue producer for the

investment dollar is the luxury loge box. While I was with the Miami Dolphins, I had devised a plan whereby the return from the rental of these boxes would be used to build a new stadium. Construction began on Joe Robbie Stadium in January of 1986, and nineteen months later, the $102 million facility was completed. Not a single tax dollar had been spent.

Applying this idea to LSU, loge boxes, as well as plush new VIP seating sections, could be added to Tiger Stadium, and the rental of each would generate enough money to pay for a unique, all-sports athletic complex which would be a part of the stadium expansion itself.

The expansion would occur in two phases. The first phase would be a renovation of the stadium's West Side, which would feature twelve luxury loge boxes, Executive Club seating for 350, concessions areas, restrooms, new press box facilities and storage areas.

The second and most extensive phase would be a massive, ten-story structure which would encompass the entire East Side of the stadium. It would feature sixty loge boxes and Club-Level seating for 2,000. In its unique design, the East Side expansion would also house all Athletic Department administrative and coaching offices, living quarters for all 300 LSU scholarship athletes (including dorm rooms, kitchen, cafeteria, study halls and study areas), sports-therapy and weight-training facilities, locker and dressing rooms, a gift shop, a ticket sales area, an LSU sports Hall of Fame and a spacious, atrium-like Sky Lobby, located adjacent to the Club-Level seating section.

Each of the project's seventy-two glass-enclosed loge boxes would measure seventeen feet across by twenty-eight feet deep. Each would be air-conditioned and heated and would feature such amenities as a private restroom, kitchenette, closed-circuit television, theater-style chairs, conversation area, a private entrance and two private parking spaces. Each loge would be available on a ten-year lease basis for $30,000 per year.

The Executive Club seats, also available on a ten-year lease basis, would be located on the West Side's fifty-yard line.

They, too, would offer glass-enclosed, air-conditioned and heated comfort as well as closed-circuit TV and access to private restrooms and a concession area. The cost of each Executive Club seat would be a one-time payment of $4,000, then $400 per year for ten years. The Club-Level seats, located on the lowest of the East Side's three new seating levels, would also be in a glass-enclosed, air-conditioned and heated viewing area with theater-style seats, closed-circuit TV monitors, concessions areas, restrooms and access to the Sky Lobby. The cost per seat would be $3,000 as a one-time payment, plus $300 per year for ten years.

The first person I contacted regarding the feasibility of my plan was Ted Jones, a brilliant Baton Rouge attorney whom I had met while setting up the Athletic Department's fund-raising arm, Tigers Unlimited, as a non-profit corporation. Jones, whose tax expertise sets him head and shoulders above the majority of the legal beagles I had dealt with, thought the idea would fly and agreed to research its tax ramifications.

Eight years earlier, Jones' knowledge of the tax code had proved invaluable to a group of football ticket purchasers. The new Upper Deck at Tiger Stadium included a section of premium seats. For a customer to be guaranteed the right to purchase one of these seats each year for ten years, he was required to pay a $1,500 option. Jones saw to it that the option was ruled a "contribution," thus allowing the customer to claim it as a tax deduction. Eight years later, the precedent still stood for allowing customers to write off a significant portion of the cost of the loge boxes, as well as the entire $3,000 and $4,000 options on the VIP seats.

Tigers Unlimited, already in place for the purpose of raising funds for athletic scholarships as well as for the renovation, improvement and construction of athletic facilities, could be used to finance and construct the Stadium Project. Because it would raise money in the private sector, this non-profit corporation would not be subjected to the state's prevailing wage and public bid laws, resulting in a savings of about $5 million on the $27-million project.

From the beginning, Jones predicted that one of two things would happen. Either the project would be a rousing success, or the state's political structure would revolt against it, and I'd be eaten alive. Care to venture an early guess as to which came to pass?

The first obstacle in my path was the Chancellor and his pride of authorship. As I had discovered over the years, if Wharton couldn't claim an idea as his own, he'd come up with a hundred reasons why it couldn't be done.

I'd also discovered that one of the best defenses against Wharton's negative posturings was a two-fisted offense. If one of my ideas bore the endorsement of someone Wharton respected and/or feared, it usually stood a much better chance of winning his initial approval. In this instance, I called upon the help of my friend Doug Manship, whom Wharton feared more, perhaps, than anyone else.

Manship expressed enthusiastic support for the Stadium Project and agreed to be present when I introduced it to Wharton. Jones said he'd be there, as well.

I invited the Chancellor to my office, telling him I wanted to make a presentation of a new idea. I forgot to mention that we wouldn't be alone.

Triple-teamed, Wharton listened quietly, and at the meeting's conclusion, I felt confident that I had at least bought enough time to mount a public relations campaign and gain the support of both the fans and the local business community. Once word was out that LSU would soon have the finest athletic facilities in the nation — and they wouldn't cost the taxpayers of Louisiana a dime to build — I'd be home free. Or so I thought.

I wouldn't find out until later that my two powerful allies had merely helped me to win a skirmish. The real war was yet to begin.

Step two in seeing my project implemented was gaining the approval of the Board of Supervisors. I made my formal presentation at the Board's January 25, 1985, meeting, and I walked away to the sound of hearty applause. "Now you see what kind of Athletic Director we have," one Board member was heard to say during a recess.

Of course, the project had its detractors. Beychok, as I've stated earlier, opposed it because he said it would divert funds from academics to athletics. Former Governor John McKeithen, with whom I had butted heads a year earlier over my decision to fire Jerry Stovall, opposed it because he said ". . . the idea of the very wealthy looking down over the masses is something that rubs me the wrong way." I'm not sure why Charles Cusimano opposed it, unless it was simply to keep his string of negative votes intact.

While the overwhelming support of the Board buoyed my confidence, Wharton's lukewarm demeanor aroused my suspicions. He didn't oppose the idea in his comments to the Board, but an endorsement was conspicuously missing. It wasn't long after that when he apparently influenced Charlie Roberts and Bill Arnsparger to undermine my plan.

Another of my well-documented adversaries, the Ethics Commission, got into the act. The commission initiated an investigation of Tigers Unlimited and eventually determined that no person serving as an employee of LSU or on the Board of Supervisors would be allowed to sit on the board of Tigers Unlimited. As a result, I was forced to resign my position as Executive Director of the very corporation that I had planned to use to build the Stadium Project. How on earth would the independent board the commission ordered implement my plan without my daily input and expertise? How was my project supposed to come about when ". . . caution should be exercised . . . by all concerned to ensure that the actions and activities of Mr. Brodhead do not inadvertently convey to the public, the press or the Commission that Mr. Brodhead has reassumed some official role in the administration of the affairs of TUC (Tigers Unlimited Corporation)."?

How ridiculous can one group of people get?

Allow me to attempt to shed further light on the commission's opposition to the project.

To finance the bulk of the work involved, Tigers Unlimited had planned to issue tax-exempt bonds through the Louisiana Public Facilities Authority. The LPFA is required to take all such requests for debt financing before the State Bonding Commission, which, in turn, determines whether the project requesting funding shall be classified as private or public works.

Public works must comply with the state's prevailing wage law, which requires contractors to pay laborers at the higher, union-contracted pay scales in a given area.

Victor Bussie, the president of the Louisiana AFL-CIO, who would naturally possess a vested interest in seeing all projects classified as public works, sits on the State Bonding Commission.

So much for objective determinations.

By the way, Bussie also happens to be a member of the Ethics Commission, my nemesis during my entire tenure as Athletic Director of LSU.

If I might digress just another moment here, I'd like to recount an incident which proved to me just how prominent a position Bussie holds on the Ethics Commission.

On March 19, 1985, I was the guest speaker at a dinner meeting of the Pelican Chapter of the Associated Builders and Contractors, Inc. During the time I was Athletic Director, I was asked to speak to literally hundreds of groups and organizations. I always spoke on the same topic, LSU athletics, and I never charged these groups a speaker's fee.

Shortly after this particular speaking engagement, I was notified by the Ethics Commission that my appearance was under investigation. Why, I had no idea. That is, until I learned that ABC is one of the most vocal lobbying groups against Louisiana's prevailing wage law.

When Jones learned that the Ethics Commission had issued its findings against Tigers Unlimited, he called a strategical retreat and, with the invaluable help of Monroe businessman Bill Boles Jr., American Bank of Monroe President

Kent Anderson, and former LSU Board of Supervisors member Johnny Sherrouse, also of Monroe, formed Louisiana Academics and Athletics, Inc. This independent, non-profit entity was created for one reason: to fund and construct my project. LAAI would rely on conventional bank loans, rather than the tax-exempt revenue bonds that Tigers Unlimited had planned to use, to finance the work, ensuring its private venture status.

The ten-year contracts signed by the purchasers of the loge boxes and VIP seats would be the only collateral required to guarantee the loans, and no mortgages would ever be placed on the properties, which LAAI would donate to the university upon completion.

After several trips to New Orleans and Dallas, we had formed a consortium of Louisiana and Texas bank executives who were very enthusiastic about our proposal. The new financial package was ready for placement.

Just when it seemed safe to get back into the water, the AFL-CIO, along with a group entitled Common Cause, filed a lawsuit against the LSU Board of Supervisors challenging the legality of building a private project on public property without the insertion of prevailing wage.

Fran (Mrs. Victor) Bussie was named as one of the parties filing the suit.

A *Morning Advocate* editorial (October 29, 1986) said of this latest development:

"It seems to us such connections raise a question of conflict of interest, if not ethics, in themselves."

Nevertheless, the demise of my project had begun, a project which would have vaulted LSU to the forefront of the intercollegiate athletic world. I was proud of my ambitious plan, not only because of what it would have meant to the Athletic Department, but because of the significant annual contributions it would have made to the university's academic side. If LAAI had received even eighty percent of the revenues we projected the project would generate, the university stood to collect approximately $796,000 a year for academic purposes. At one hundred percent, the university would receive about $920,000 a year. Once the debt on the project was retired, academics could have gained up to $1.6 million a year!

In light of the recent budget cuts the university finds itself faced with, wouldn't my project have been a revenue producer worth fighting for?

I was also proud that my plan would not have involved the university's credit in any way. Nor would the faith and credit of the state have been needed to float this indebtedness. Last but not least, not a dime of taxpayers' money would have been needed to bring this far-reaching concept to fruition.

As I stated at the beginning of this chapter, hindsight has shed a great deal of light on why the Stadium Project was doomed from the beginning.

In my opinion:

— Wharton opposed it because its success would have meant that athletics, Brodhead-style, was here to stay. It would also have meant the end of his master plan to control the Athletic Department from his office on the hill.

— Bussie opposed it because a public facility built with private money on public land, exempt from higher, union wages, would have set a dangerous precedent. Had my plan slipped through a crack in organized labor's stranglehold on the state, the taxpayers may have finally realized that prevailing wage is one of the primary reasons that many industries avoid Louisiana like the plague.

— Beychok opposed it because a Brodhead-authored success story of this magnitude would have caused irreparable damage to his athletic-dependent power base.

— Roberts opposed it because he couldn't afford for the Athletic Department to contribute more money to the university on an annual basis than he could raise among the alumni.

— Arnsparger opposed it because, as I had come to find out, he wanted to be LSU's next Athletic Director. Had my

134

project succeeded, that would have been impossible.

Ironically, my adversaries had used my project to ensure my downfall. Not only did they eventually succeed in getting rid of me, they also lost for LSU an opportunity that may never come again.

In the face of the new federal tax law which prohibited writing off lease payments made on loge boxes and premium seats, Jones had single-handedly lobbied the Congress of the United States to grandfather LSU's tax-exempt status. Much to Jones' credit, only one other school, the University of Texas, was included in this special ruling.

There was a catch, however. Word was out in Washington that the provision would be revoked at the end of the 1986 tax year and that if LSU was to slip in under the wire, prompt action was required. In other words, the time to start the project was then. But my critics were too busy with what the *Morning Advocate* called "political posturing and sour grapes directed at Brodhead personally" to heed the warnings. The deadline came and went.

In the end, the ship sailed, and, once again, LSU was left standing on the dock.

CHAPTER EIGHT

Stung by
a Bug

For years, the LSU Athletic Department had suffered as the result of sensitive matters being leaked to the media.

Because of the fervent public interest focused on LSU athletics, every bit of information emanating from the Athletic Department was subjected to intense scrutiny. When the information appeared out of context or without explanation, the result was oftentimes a public debate, accompanied by a great deal of misinterpretation and confusion.

Public relations is an important part of successfully running a business such as the LSU Athletic Department. Timing is crucial. Positive marketing strategies released after the details of a project or negotiation have been bandied about in the media usually prove anticlimactic. Add to that the ever-present danger that controversy is fair game in the "recruiting wars," and information leaks can be devastating.

I suspected this problem had begun long before I arrived at LSU. It was apparently in full swing during the Dietzel administration, as evidenced by the following transcript. I stumbled upon it, written on a folded piece of paper, when I was cleaning out my desk after tendering my resignation on October 21, 1986. It had been concealed these years beneath a collapsed metal drawer separator.

"TAPES"

"1. Press Conference Tapes — Sources? Newell, Kalivoda, Calhoun, ???

"2. Tapes of Board of Supervisors — Sources? Mrs. Strain, Dr. Woodin? PR office?

"3. Tapes of Telephone Conversations — Dietzel's phone? Gilmore's phone? Chancellor's phone? Phone of someone in media? Phone of some member of Board? Someone else's phone? Whose?

"4. Concealed on-person recorded tapes? Possible, but who?"

"SABOTAGE"

"1. Leak of Stadium repair story

"2. Raise questions at Legislative auditor about LSU Foundation

"3. Make snide accusations to IRS

"4. Turn LSU in to the NCAA

"5. Leak of expense of Board members on trips

"6. Examination of relationships between Board and those who receive Board scholarships."

I was astounded by my bizarre discovery, and while not everything on the list made sense, most of it was only too clear. I looked through the Athletic Department files for a handwritten note which might lead me to the author, but I found nothing.

Studying the list more closely, item (6) in particular, I recalled an article which had appeared in the local Sunday newspaper less than two months earlier. Entitled "Need, Ability, Politics Decide Who Gets Help From LSU Board," the story revealed that some Board of Supervisors members admitted to being influenced by "politics and pull" when awarding special Board-sponsored scholarships. It revealed to me that either somebody was a very good prognosticator, or the "Master Plan" detailed above was still alive and well.

By the beginning of 1985, information was being leaked out of the Athletic Department with such regularity that I discontinued the practice of staff meetings. I was suspect of nearly everyone in my office, and I began to form a close cadre of staff members to assist me in the decision-making process.

I trusted my secretary, Pat Dale, who knew as much as anyone about the innerworkings of the Athletic Department, as well as the handpicked advisors with whom I had surrounded myself. Other than that, I had taken to attaching a small piece of scotch tape from my door to the door frame when I left at night, in hopes of discovering if someone was sneaking into my office after hours. Kay called the phone company and had our home phone swept for bugs. The same thing was done to my office phone. Nothing in the way of recording or listening devices was found.

My frustration was quickly giving way to preoccupation. I wanted the Judas goats who were violating the sanctity of the Athletic Department. And I wanted them yesterday. To make matters worse, the Chancellor was on my back about the "looseness" of my department.

I am an imaginative person by nature, and if there was any tightening up to be done, I'd find a way to do it. One can imagine the variety of ideas flying through the chopper as I attempted to hit on one foolproof plan to nab the offenders.

Basketball Coach Dale Brown fueled the fires by constantly showing me the variety of recording devices he kept in his office. He had been using the equipment to tape incoming phone calls from his former players who were being questioned by the NCAA about the LSU basketball program. I didn't need that type of equipment, since taping telephone conversations wasn't going to help me catch the leak. But placing some sort of recording device in my office might. If I could tell a different but sensational story to each of the people of whom I was suspicious, then sit back and wait until one of the stories appeared in the media, I'd have my leak.

And I'd have the proof on tape.

I didn't know what kind of equipment I'd need towards that end, and I didn't know where I'd go to get it. Brown, whom I often likened to the TV detective Columbo, told me that a friend of his, Dick Barrios, was an expert in debugging — and possibly vice versa — endeavors.

After Barrios and I made several unsuccessful attempts to get together, Brown arranged for a meeting between us. Barrios came to my office and swept it for bugs. While he was there, I expressed to him my concern with the information leak as well as my desire to invent a way to "smoke out the snake." Barrios told me he'd look into it and get back with me.

Several weeks passed, and I'd nearly put the matter out of my mind when Barrios called and told me he couldn't handle the equipment I'd need but that he knew someone who could. He said he'd arrange a meeting between George Davis and me the next time Davis came to town.

Had I known what I was flirting with, and with whom I was about to become associated, I'd have called time out, looked to the big press box in the sky and asked someone for help.

Davis is a short, heavy man with a high-pitched voice. He's also an FBI informant whose specialties include the taping of conversations with concealed body wires and the delivery of recording equipment, complete with FBI agents hiding in the bushes to observe the transfer.

To me, Davis was simply someone, recommended by a friend of a friend, who might help me catch the person who was hurting my Athletic Department.

After initial contact was made with a phone call, Davis visited me at my office to find out what I wanted to accomplish and to survey the physical layout. He told me he'd think about what type of equipment I'd need and come up with something.

The course Davis was to follow over the next several weeks is unclear to me, but since he works for pay in these transactions, I must assume he reported, after leaving my

office, to whomever had hired him. Did he then go to the FBI
to inform them of what I was planning? Did the FBI then
assume control of the operation?

Just about the time that my plan was taking shape, the
NCAA intensified its investigation of the basketball program.
Nearly three years had passed since the inquiry into both the
football and basketball programs began, and NCAA investigator Doug Johnson had been in town on numerous occasions to question LSU athletes and former athletes on a
variety of subjects.

Johnson, an attorney by trade, had already carved one
SEC notch in his belt by directing the investigation of the
University of Florida football program which resulted in a
number of severe sanctions. My friend Bill Carr, then Athletic
Director at Florida, had warned me that Johnson was
"unscrupulous," and that "he'd stop at nothing to prove his
case." Carr also told me that Johnson had used "questionable, if not outright unethical" investigatory tactics during his
Florida probe. In fact, there were stories circulating around
the SEC that Florida Head Football Coach Charlie Pell threw a
book at Johnson during one particularly grueling interroga-
tion.

Johnson was very good at putting whomever he
talked to on the defensive with his "I'm only doing my job"
routine. During his introductory meeting with Wharton, the
two nearly came to blows in my presence when Johnson
challenged LSU's integrity.

Dale Brown wasn't among Johnson's fans, either.
Daily, Brown would show me transcripts of the taped conversations he'd had with former LSU basketball player Steffond Johnson, who had since enrolled at San Diego State and
was being questioned by the NCAA's Johnson.

The transcripts contained Steffond Johnson's de-
scriptions of the meals and drinks bought for him by the
NCAA's Johnson, as well as veiled and unveiled threats the
latter had made when he questioned the player about the

LSU program. It was apparent to me that the NCAA's Johnson was trying to induce Steffond Johnson into pointing the finger of guilt at Brown and his assistant coaches. Page after transcript page detailed what I considered to be unethical investigatory methods, and I was soon conditioned to attack Doug Johnson at the first sign of coercion.

After several years of conducting off-campus interviews, Johnson began his questioning sessions with current LSU athletes. These interviews were conducted in my office, and, according to NCAA policy, I was allowed to be present when the investigator questioned the athletes about their own school.

I had a problem with the fact that months would pass between the time the interrogations took place and the time when Johnson would present the athletes with a document containing the statements they were supposed to have made during the interviews. The athletes were asked to sign the report with nothing more than my handwritten notes for reference.

I had taken fairly good notes during the interview sessions, but I knew they weren't enough to help the athletes recall the context in which their remarks had been made. They were certainly lacking when one considers that the athletes' signatures could ultimately be used to affect their eligibility. Something needed to be done to protect the athletes.

In addition, I was asked to leave my office when Johnson wanted to question the athlete about an institution other than LSU. Tito Horford, the recently recruited 7'1" freshman from the Dominican Republic, was being questioned extensively by Johnson, and I was often asked to excuse myself from the proceedings. I was reluctant to leave Horford, whose comprehension of the English language was limited, despite the fact that I had been allowed to bring in one of the university's Spanish instructors to act as interpreter.

On this particular afternoon, Brown came roaring into my office to tell me that Horford had just admitted that

Johnson questioned him about LSU after I had been asked to leave, in an apparent violation of NCAA procedures.

At that moment, I thought of the recording equipment I was contemplating for my office. At that same moment, I formed what the courts would later label "intent."

I was under a great deal of pressure at this time to maintain the steady progress the athletic program had enjoyed during the previous two years. As the 1985-86 school year began, LSU had a legitimate shot at winning the Bernie Moore Trophy, significant of the best men's athletic program in the Southeastern Conference, for just the second time in the thirteen-year history of the prestigious award. I was also anxious to see my Five Year Plan to establish a successful, broad-based athletic program bear fruit a little early. The last thing I needed was more delays in the NCAA's already drawn-out investigation. If I could catch Johnson interrogating our athletes using procedures which were inconsistent with NCAA policies, I would head for NCAA headquarters in Mission, Kan., and put an end to the whole thing, once and for all.

My reason for wanting to install recording equipment in my office had just become two-fold: I wanted to stop the damaging leak of information, and I wanted to safeguard the LSU athletes against unfair methods of questioning. My ultimate goal, however, remained singular: LSU was being hurt, and I was going to do everything in my power to protect it.

At this point, however, Davis was beginning to arouse my suspicion. Our phone conversations, always initiated by him, were becoming more and more frequent. His salesmanship was growing in intensity. And he always called me from out of town.

Curious, I did a little investigating. I already suspected that some bugging and wiretapping was illegal, but I wanted to find out why the kind of recording that Brown was doing was not. I learned that the recording of conversations is illegal only if none of the parties involved knows that a recording is being made. I had planned to cover that requirement in both instances: The athlete being questioned would know, in case I was asked to leave the room, that the equipment was being used, and I would know the recording was being made as I planted my false stories with my leak suspects.

Yet I allowed Davis' behavior to confuse me, and I couldn't shake the feeling that something about my plan, perhaps the equipment itself, wasn't right. Despite my knowledge to the contrary, Davis tricked me into expressing my doubts out loud. On at least one occasion, while I was unknowingly being taped by Davis, I was enticed into admitting that what I intended to do was illegal. That utterance was to later become the only evidence which the government had in its case against me.

Shortly after Johnson's questioning of Horford, the Athletic Department attorney and I challenged Johnson that the athletes were being denied due process when they were refused access to the investigator's notes. We requested permission for a court reporter to be present, which the NCAA denied. We persisted, and finally, Johnson notified me that athletes being interrogated would be permitted to have an attorney present, and that the attorney would be allowed to remain in the room, regardless of the line of questioning.

That bit of information effectively ended my need for the recording equipment as far as catching Johnson went. I had still hoped to catch the person who was leaking Athletic Department information, but I was losing interest, perhaps because of the doubts Davis had instilled in my mind, in using recording equipment to do it. In addition, the sports year was now in full swing, and my attention had been diverted by its never-ending demands on my time.

Davis wasn't through with me yet, however, and he escalated his sales campaign. In retrospect, it seems that Davis knew I had been granted permission for an attorney to be present with the athletes and that my need for and interest in the recording equipment was ebbing. He pressed on, even as I became less and less attentive to his carefully conceived dialogue. When I was later allowed to review the transcripts made of our conversations, I was embarrassed by my curt, thoughtless responses.

Undeterred, Davis called me during the week of October 14 to arrange a time during the upcoming weekend when he could deliver the equipment. I half-heartedly agreed to meet him that Friday night, forgetting I had already agreed to make an appearance at a local department store's Homecoming Weekend celebration. When Friday evening arrived, I had reached such a level of disinterest in the equipment that I stood up Davis.

I hoped my no-show would put an end to this unilateral relationship, but it didn't.

The following week, Davis called again and told me that he had gone to a lot of trouble to get the equipment and that the least I could do was take it off his hands.

He had finally succeeded in pushing the right button. I felt guilty for putting him through all that trouble. I didn't know what I was going to do with the equipment once I got it, but I agreed to meet him that Saturday night, an open date for the football team.

At about 10:30 p.m. on October 26, Davis called me at home and told me to meet him at my office. At about 11 p.m., I arrived and parked my car in the darkened stadium lot. I walked to the front door of the Athletic Department offices and began to unlock it, when Davis approached. He asked me to walk with him to his truck, where he had the equipment. The report filed by the FBI agents who were hidden in the bushes would read that I was observed carrying Davis' briefcase into my office. The fat bastard had asked me to carry it because he said he had a bad back.

Once inside, Davis unwrapped the equipment and set it up for an audio test. I was surprised at the simplicity of what he had, having been led to believe that the components were highly technical, illegal or both. Davis' equipment could have been, and probably was, purchased at the local Radio Shack. None of it, as far as I could determine, would have been classified as illegal.

He set up the receiver in an office adjacent to mine to

determine whether or not the signals would penetrate the interior walls. He didn't tie in the small recorder for the final test, however, because I didn't have any tapes.

No tapes. How's that for the criminal mind at work?

When Davis was through with the setup, I told him to disassemble the equipment and put it back in the box. He looked surprised, especially when I told him to put the box in my lower left-hand desk drawer.

I knew I'd never be able to put it all back together again, but it didn't matter. I knew I'd never use it.

When he'd put the box in the drawer, Davis asked me for $375. As usual, I wasn't carrying any cash, and I told him I didn't have it. He told me that I could leave the money with Barrios, and that he'd get it the next time he saw him. I would later see a transcript of a conversation between Barrios and Davis in which Davis said that I hadn't paid him yet, but he would "make me for more later." Was blackmail also a part of this operation?

Looking back, I recall Brown telling me that his friend was an electronic equipment expert. If Barrios was such an authority, why call in Davis, especially to handle such simple equipment?

When Kay awoke the next morning with a sinus head-ache, we decided not to go to church. She thought she'd feel better if she went back to bed for a while, so while she rested, I drove over to the office to pick up some paperwork.

It was approximately 10 a.m. when I arrived at the Athletic Department, and not forty-five minutes later when I left for home.

As I pulled into my driveway and stopped my car, a second vehicle turned in and parked immediately behind me. A third vehicle quickly pulled across the end of the driveway, blocking the road. Two men jumped out of the lead car, identifying themselves as FBI agents.

There are no words to express my shock. I had no idea why they were there, but I felt certain they hadn't come for coffee. They began to question me about the surveillance equipment I had in my office. They wanted to know about my association with George Davis. What had I done with the tapes? Was I going to cooperate with the search warrant they were waving under my nose?

I was so confused by their arrival that "the tapes" question didn't register until much later. What tapes? The search warrant the agent showed me already listed a typed description of each piece of equipment to be found. If they knew what they were looking for, why the pretense about the tapes?

The equipment had been delivered twelve hours earlier, and it had never left my desk drawer. Surely the FBI, as involved as they obviously were in the sting, knew that I hadn't used the equipment between 11 p.m. Saturday and 11 a.m. Sunday. In the first place, at those hours, who was I going to record? Secondly, without tapes, the equipment didn't work.

Naturally, I cooperated fully with the agents and accompanied them to my office, where I insisted they remove the equipment from my desk. For the next hour, each piece was carefully checked and photographed. In retrospect, I wonder if this was done to give the TV cameras time to arrive.

I would find out later that the weekend crews from the television stations WAFB and WBRZ had been on the scene an hour earlier, but apparently, they had gotten their signals crossed. Instead of heading for the Athletic Director's office, the crew members went to the football office, located around the corner. Two assistant coaches later told me that the reporters had come into the office and said they'd received a tip that a big bust was about to come down. They wanted to know if the coaches had seen "any FBI men hanging around."

Also later, I asked Doug Manship, who owns WBRZ, to inquire of his news director how the tip had occurred. The news director told Manship that the staff had "intercepted a radio transmission" and dispatched a crew to check it out. While I didn't believe the story, it did serve to add a twist of irony to the whole episode. The United States government was to eventually find me guilty of the petty offense which reads "conspiracy to intercept radio communications."

While the FBI agents searched my office, another group of agents was paying the Chancellor a visit at his home. He never did explain to me the purpose of their house call, but that didn't surprise me. He also never explained to me a statement he made to Manship nearly a year later regarding the bugging incident.

According to a "To Whom It May Concern" letter Manship gave me to use in my defense, if needed, before the NCAA Infractions Committee: "Chancellor Wharton and I (Manship) talked about the whole affair, and then I said to Chancellor Wharton, 'You know, the whole bugging affair was a frame-up and should not have happened.' Chancellor Wharton replied that for two weeks before the bugging incident came out into the open, the FBI stonewalled all attempts to call the whole thing off. I was amazed at this statement, but I made no reply."

I hesitate to guess at what the Chancellor's involvement, if any, was in the operation. At this point, nothing would surprise me.

For three-and-a-half years, I had managed to stay out in front of the posse by using wit, guile and the basic will to survive. Wins and profits had been my protective shield. But I had forgotten to protect my flanks.

My enemies had been waiting a long time for me to slip, and slip I finally did. It didn't matter that it was on a perfectly placed banana peel.

CHAPTER NINE

The United States of America vs. Robert E. Brodhead

The local news media often referred to the years I spent at LSU as "the stormy, tumultuous tenure of Bob Brodhead." If that assessment is an accurate one, then no time was more stormy or tumultuous than the period between October 27, 1985, when the FBI seized the recording equipment George Davis had brought to my office, and October 8, 1986, when Jim Wharton had accumulated what he considered to be sufficient evidence to suspend me from my job.

When the FBI agents left my office on that October morning in 1985, I got into my car and headed for home. I was shocked by the events of the past few hours, and a hundred questions were racing through my mind.

Had I been arrested? No, I couldn't have been. No one had read me my rights.

Were those men really FBI agents? They had to be, but one of them smelled like the bottom of an oak barrel in a Jack Daniels distillery.

What was the conservative LSU faculty going to think when "FBI Searches Athletic Director's Office; Recording Equipment Found" hit the newsstands?

Had I done anything that might be considered a federal offense?

The minute I got home, I picked up the telephone to call the Chancellor and braced myself for the explosion I knew would come from the other end of the line. To my great surprise, Wharton was not only calm and collected, he was also very sympathetic. He advised me to call Camille Gravel, a noted Louisiana attorney and one of the Board of Supervisors' reigning monarchs.

Gravel, who had already been apprised of the situation by Wharton, recommended that I engage the services of James Boren, a local criminal attorney.

If you've never been surprised on an otherwise routine Sunday morning by a bunch of FBI agents asking questions that might lead to some very serious criminal charges, I don't recommend it. In the field of athletics, I am, as a local sportswriter once wrote, "a supremely self-confident man." In the field of criminal law, I'm a duck out of water.

My fear and confusion must have come through loud and clear when I called Boren that evening and tried desperately to relate the day's events without succumbing to a severe panic attack. He listened, consoled and told me he'd take the case. He also told me to try and collect myself.

I don't remember if we actually got together later that evening or early the following morning, but our first face-to-face meeting was devoted to discussing legal as well as public relations strategies. We knew we needed time to develop a game plan, and Boren was going to make every effort to have the results of the search warrant sealed. For some reason, this could not be accomplished, and the documentation became public record.

One of the first members of the media to request a copy was Steve Myers, publisher of *Tiger Rag*.

Myers had long since taken to printing such blatantly negative things about me and my administration that Kay wouldn't allow the publication through the door of our home. From what I could gather, a growing number of Tiger fans felt the same way. Daily, I heard from former subscribers who told me they had grown tired of his antagonistic reporting.

To provide fans with a positive picture of LSU athletics, I had previously created an internally produced, newsletter-type publication called *Tiger Tracks*. Subtitled the "Official Voice of LSU Sports," *Tiger Tracks* offered news and features about the entire athletic program, and the response of the community was very positive.

In 1986, Myers came to me and offered to sell *Tiger Rag* to the Athletic Department. He said he was thinking about entering law school but wanted to sell his paper before making a final decision. His asking price was $500,000.

During one of his visits, Myers showed me his most recent financial statement. It reflected a profit which, in my opinion, was insufficient to cover his liabilities, among which were some fairly hefty equipment notes.

I decided against purchasing the paper for two reasons: I didn't consider it a good business prospect, and *Tiger Tracks* was beginning to thrive.

Myers would eventually threaten to take the matter of the Athletic Department's publication before the state Legislature. He claimed that *Tiger Tracks* was a product of the public sector, and as such, held an unfair advantage in its competition with his privately produced newspaper. In reality, I didn't consider the papers to be competitors.

Tiger Tracks was a public relations tool, created for the purpose of promoting all eighteen of LSU's sports teams. It didn't accept advertising, so it wasn't competing with *Tiger Rag* for the advertising dollar. In addition, *Tiger Tracks* was striving to become self-sufficient. Thanks to a steadily growing subscribers' list and a plan whereby Tigers Unlimited had agreed to purchase a subscription for each of its Satellite Club members, *Tiger Tracks* would have become self-sustaining in its second year of existence.

Myers' threat succeeded in scaring Wharton, however, and he ordered that *Tiger Tracks* cease publication.

Wharton justified its demise by calling the paper an economic liability. Not only had he ignored our projections for *Tiger Tracks'* financial future, he had apparently neglected to assign any value to the positive image it had painted of the Athletic Department and its many accomplishments.

The story of the FBI's search of my office hit the media, and a frightening series of events unfolded in rapid succession. Boren, his law partner, Lennie Perez, and Athletic Department Public Relations Consultant Gus Weill decided a press conference was in order, and we set to work on the statement I would make. We determined that in it, I should describe 1) my desire to catch the person or persons responsible for the information leaks emanating from the Athletic Department and 2) the events which had caused me to believe that the NCAA investigator may have been questioning LSU athletes in a manner inconsistent with NCAA policy.

When a draft of the release was presented to Wharton for his approval, however, he vetoed the mention of the NCAA, saying that such a disclosure might upset the timetable of the ongoing probe. It was determined that I should reveal my concern with uncovering the leak, add a statement which said, "I additionally wished to have the equipment to preserve accurate records of other important discussions that take place in my office," and leave it at that.

For the first time in my LSU career, I appeared before the media a frightened man. What a horrible feeling to face these people without my usual cocksure self-confidence.

I had always been brutally honest with the media, and I knew the reporters on hand would expect no less from me now. My attorneys, however, had urged me to be very careful with what I said. I had yet to be charged, and they warned me that anything I said might ultimately endanger my case.

I approached the podium fighting the urge to divulge the whole wretched story . . . the set-up artist . . . the persistent phone calls . . . telling Davis to put the equipment in my desk drawer because I knew I'd never use it . . . the sting itself. Instead, I forced myself to read the carefully worded statement we had prepared, and when I finished, I refused to answer any questions. Like the little boy at the dike, I had my finger stuck in the hole. But in my fairy tale, no one called me a hero. I left the room before I said something my attorneys would regret.

Next, a federal grand jury was convened, and I was the "unannounced target." My attorneys suggested that rather than wait to be subpoenaed, I should appear voluntarily.

Grand juries are an interesting function of our judicial system. They are composed of up to twenty-four members who hear testimony from all concerned parties, then decide whether there is sufficient evidence of wrongdoing to warrant the handing down of indictments. Persons who testify do so under the questioning of the prosecuting attorneys; attorneys for the defense are not present. In addition, the target of a grand jury probe is not permitted to review the testimony of the other witnesses or to comment on the validity of what has been said.

Wharton, Dale Brown, University Attorney Mike Pharis and, reportedly, George Davis testified before the grand jury looking into my case. What any of them said remains a mystery to me.

My testimony lasted two hours, during which time I was questioned by several assistant U.S. Attorneys. It was a terrifying experience, but I had been well coached by Boren and Perez. I told the grand jury the truth as I recollected it to be, and I could tell by the look in the jurymen's eyes that they believed me. I left the courthouse believing that the session had gone as well as could be expected.

While FBI Special Agent Jerry Phipps was pushing for an indictment, U.S. Attorney Stanford O. Bardwell was privately expressing his doubts to several mutual acquaintances regarding the strength of the FBI's case. In fact, one friend told me that Bardwell believed that were it not for the national publicity which the *Sports Illustrated* article had created in November, the entire matter may very well have "dried up and blown away."

As it was, my fate rested in the hands of my attorneys and the federal prosecutors, and it would take all the strength and courage my family and I could muster to make it through the long months ahead.

The strain of maintaining a positive public facade was exhausting, and my daily sessions at my attorneys' office, spent reliving every painful detail, left me drained. I awakened in the middle of many a night, drenched with sweat. In my recurring nightmare, a judge whose face I did not know would tell me that I wasn't going to see my family for a long, long time because he was sending me to prison. When I'd beg him to tell me what I'd done, he'd just smile. Some nights, he'd laugh, too.

On campus, I received a great deal of support. Many members of the university community called to tell me to hang in there, and the majority of my staff stood behind me with heart-warming loyalty. Arnsparger, as I've detailed, chose to do the opposite, and several of my administrative assistants aligned themselves with the power base developing in the football office. The wavering allegiance of those whom I had trusted, at a time when I needed all the moral support I could get, hurt me deeply.

Predictably, a few members of the university faculty called for my resignation, as did several student organizations. Shortly after the story broke, a "Brodhead Bugs the Students, Too" banner was prominently displayed during the LSU-Alabama football game, and "Bugs Brodhead" tee shirts, bearing a caricature of me eating a carrot, could be seen around campus. My younger daughter Amy, who had transferred to LSU from the University of Georgia the year before, came home one evening in tears, carrying the remnants of a "Brodhead Bugs Me" bumper sticker she had torn from a classmate's car.

The LSU student body had held me in collective disregard for some time, having been led to believe that I was responsible for the loss of some 600 seats from the student section in Tiger Stadium. In actuality, Wharton, who had taken a great deal of heat from a number of state legislators because he had taken away their complimentary football tickets, needed to come up with replacements. At the same time, I needed to find a little more than 100 tickets to sell to a group of local businessmen who employed LSU athletes during the summer months. In a three-way decision, Wharton, Roberts and I determined that since the student section was averaging about 2,000 no-shows per game, the seats we needed would best be taken from that area of the stadium.

When the time came to release the details of the arrangement to the student body, however, Wharton and Roberts were nowhere to be found. I had taken twenty percent of the tickets, but, in the end, I got 100 percent of the blame.

From the beginning of the bugging ordeal, Wharton had managed to appear supportive of me. He told the media that he shared my concern over sensitive information "being given to the outside world without the University having the opportunity to comment on the context or meaning of them." He convinced the Board of Supervisors that he was anxious for a swift and judicious conclusion to the episode and that he condoned waiting until all the facts were in before taking any official action.

Behind closed doors, however, he was singing a different tune.

On several occasions, Wharton told Boren, Perez and me that if I were indicted, he would suspend me without pay until the matter was settled. Since I couldn't afford to go a month without pay, let alone the ten months to a year the Justice Department was predicting it might need to bring the matter to trial, the Chancellor's promised intentions caused me a great deal of anxiety.

In retrospect, Wharton's threat to suspend me on the grounds of an indictment was tantamount to finding me guilty until proven innocent. Apparently, President Copping disapproved of such disregard for due process, for when Wharton told him of his plans, Copping balked. In fact, Copping would later tell me that he had informed Wharton, in no uncertain terms, that he *could not* suspend me. Wharton, however, decided to withhold that bit of information from me, choosing instead to hold the threat of suspension without pay over my head like a guillotine. Many of the decisions I was to make over the course of the next few months were based on my belief that Wharton, indeed, would make good on his ominous warning.

Christmas came and went, and still we waited. No word was forthcoming from the grand jury, and my attorneys remained embroiled in lengthy discussions with the U.S. Attorney's office.

Then, in mid-January, the wheels began to turn with increasing speed. Bardwell, citing his close ties to LSU, announced that he had removed himself from the investigation and that the entire matter had been turned over to the Washington, D.C., headquarters of the U.S. Department of Justice. Boren and Perez made contact with government attorney James Reynolds, who had replaced Bardwell as chief federal prosecutor, and after several weeks of long-distance discussions, we were invited to Washington.

I was hopeful that being "kicked upstairs" would result in a timely disposition of the case, but I knew there were no guarantees. This was a whole new ball game, and I didn't know any of the players.

It was snowing when Boren, Perez and I checked into the Washington, D.C., Marriott on a dark afternoon in late January. It was cold, but that wasn't why I was shivering. Quite frankly, I was scared to death.

As I sat awake that night, not even bothering to try to sleep, I thought about what my family and I had been through during the past three months. I thought about the turmoil which was brewing back home in the Athletic Department: Arnsparger's threats to interview with the Tampa Bay Buccaneers if I didn't fire Dale Brown; the Ethics Commission's attacks on my Stadium Project; Beychok's vows to see me fired. And I prayed that somehow, things would get better.

The next morning, Boren and Perez left me behind at the hotel and headed for the Justice Department. There was nothing for me to do now but wait. And worry.

I called home several times just to hear Kay's voice. We made small talk and tried to hide our fears from each other, but it wasn't working. Each time I'd hang up, I'd wonder who was more frightened, she or I.

By the time my attorneys returned to the hotel for lunch, I was nearly frantic. They had spent the morning reviewing the transcripts of the taped conversations between Davis and me, they said, but other than that, nothing definite had transpired. They ate, and I asked questions, none of which were answered to my satisfaction. They finished their meals while mine sat on my plate, untouched.

After lunch, my guardians headed back to the halls of justice and told me they'd call if I was needed. I spent the afternoon in my room, pacing the floor and staring, unseeing, at the television set.

Finally, at about 4 p.m., the phone rang. Boren's voice said that it was time for me to meet them at Reynolds' office. I hailed a cab for the short, ten-minute ride. My heart was pounding so hard that the driver probably heard it.

Boren and Perez were waiting as I stepped from the elevator, and I anxiously searched their faces for some trace of good news. I found nothing, and I broke into a sweat.

As we waited for Reynolds to appear, I concentrated on breathing deeply and trying to steady my trembling hands. I had no idea what I was in for, but something told me it wasn't going to be good. Reynolds finally arrived, and after he and I were introduced, we were all ushered into a conference room nearby.

After we took our places around the table, Boren told me to review the document laying before me. I took a deep breath and picked it up.

THE UNITED STATES OF AMERICA
VS. ROBERT E. BRODHEAD

The words hit me like a baseball bat between the eyes.

Not even my worst nightmares had prepared me for the shock of that moment, for the shock of those nine words. I tried to force my eyes down the page, but they kept returning to the bold-faced declaration across the top.

Finally, I began to read the pages in my hands. Contained within was a five-count felony indictment against me, not to mention the execution notice for my athletic career.

By now, I was fighting the impulse to stand up and scream that this was all a mistake. I shouldn't be here! Can't you people see I don't belong here? Can't you see that something is terribly, terribly wrong?

"My country tis of thee, Sweet land of liberty.
"Of thee I sing."

Panic. I was beginning to panic.

Then, just as suddenly, my emotions switched gears. The more I read, the angrier I became. Listed before me were three counts of intent to commit wiretapping offenses and two drummed-up perjury charges. The government was basing its entire case on a tape-recorded conversation between Davis and me in which he asked me if I knew that what I wanted to do was illegal, and I flippantly answered, "Yeah, but what they're doing is illegal, too."

In my nonlegal mind, there wasn't a jury in the world that would hold my wise-cracking mouth against me. Surely this one statement, obtained by a crafty set-up artist, wasn't enough to convict me of five felonies.

A jury would see that I had abandoned my plan to use the equipment. I would make them understand that if I had really planned to tape record the NCAA investigator, who was scheduled to conduct his interviews in my office three days after the equipment was delivered, I would have allowed Davis, the so-called electronics expert, to set it up while he was there. They would also see that my original plan, which was to use the equipment to record my conversations with my leak suspects — conversations to which I would have been a party — was not illegal.

I had a chance after all. My hope was returning.

It didn't stay for long. Boren assured me that the

Justice Department would pursue the indictment. He also painstakingly explained to me that federal attorneys try weak cases every day. Some are won. Some are lost. But none get rained out.

By the time the meeting ended, I was numb. I had been allowed to review the transcripts of my conversations with Davis, but my emotions were on overload, and nothing was making much sense. My attorneys half led me out of the courthouse, and we headed back to the hotel.

Boren and Perez accompanied me to my room, and I collapsed onto the bed. I had never been more weary in my life.

Boren sat on the room's second bed and told me about a discussion he and the federal prosecutors had held at some point during the negotiating process. He said mention had been made of pursuing a lesser charge, but that he would need to do some research before determining if it was a viable option.

I asked what "pursuing a lesser charge" meant, and he explained that it was a complex alternative to the document I had read at the Justice Department. For all the more I understood of what he was saying, he could have been speaking Chinese. But at that point, anything sounded better than a five-count felony indictment.

Boren placed a long-distance phone call to Camille Gravel and gave him a full report of the day's activities. He also mentioned the bit about the lesser charge and told Gravel that he would be exploring it further when he got back to town. He bid Gravel good night and hung up.

Gravel, according to Boren, had reacted favorably to the news of the lesser charge. In fact, Boren said, Gravel had indicated that if research showed it to be an acceptable alternative and I should elect to follow that route, he would do whatever he could to see that the Board responded with a reprimand, nothing more. Since my greatest fear had centered around being forced to stay away from the job for any length of time, I was greatly encouraged by this sudden development. For the first time in months, I thought I saw a light at the end of the tunnel.

During the following week, Kay and I spent a great many hours discussing the options before us. I could fight, which would mean indictment, suspension without pay, another $50,000 in legal fees and the possibility of financial as well as emotional bankruptcy. It also meant the chance to clear our good name.

Or I could agree to plead guilty to a lesser charge, with the assurance of one of the Board's most influential members that he would do his best to convince his fellow Board members that a reprimand would be sufficient punishment, and hopefully, bring the matter to an end. The pain, the suffering, the emotional wear and tear on our family would be over.

I called my attorneys. With every fiber of truth and justice in my body pulling the other way, I gave the go-ahead to accept the plea bargain being offered.

The crime to which I would plead guilty, my attorneys carefully explained, was a petty offense, punishable by a maximum sentence of six months imprisonment and a $1,000 fine. The charge would state that I had conspired to intercept radio communications and "divulge the substance of such communications to others."

Radio communications? I asked. Where did that come from?

As it was explained to me, it came from the fact that Davis' little transmitter would have used radio signals to send the conversations it picked up in my office to the receiver and tape recorder which would have been installed in the office next door. That meant the whole process was classified as a radio communication, and radio communications were subject to federal laws.

My confusion aside, the plea bargaining entered its final stages, and I was finally able to spend some time enjoying the magnificent efforts being put forth by the spring sports teams. Thanks to the strong finishes being staged by the golf, track, tennis and baseball programs, LSU stood poised to win the Bernie Moore Trophy, the award given each year to the SEC's best men's athletic program, for the first time since 1979.

Equally as rewarding to me was the secondary round of approval given to my Stadium Project by the Board of Supervisors. I had worried that my personal ordeal might somehow alter the Board members' initial acceptance of my plan, and I looked upon their support as a personal vote of confidence.

Of course, I also spent a considerable amount of time dodging the bullets my adversaries sent flying my way. I was particularly taken aback by an offer made by Beychok, via his best friend, of a year's salary in return for my resignation.

The legal documents were finally proofed and signed, and my appearance before U.S. District Judge John V. Parker was set for April 18, 1986.

I arrived at Boren's office early that morning, and we made the five-minute drive to the courthouse in his car. He told me not to be nervous, that there was nothing to worry about. I knew the combined recommendations of my attorneys, the prosecutors and a probation officer had been accepted by the judge, and he would neither sentence me to jail nor place me on probation. So why was I so scared?

The courthouse steps were jammed with reporters and camera crews, and every step I took between the car and front door was filmed for the evening news. I was suddenly glad I had told Kay to stay at home.

Inside was no better, as members of the media and onlookers alike scurried for seats. I was surprised, as I made my way into the courtroom, at the number of observers who wished me luck or patted me on the back as I passed.

Several cases were called before mine, and as I listened to a drug dealer plead guilty to a rather serious charge, I closed my eyes and silently asked God, "What am I doing here?"

"The United States of America vs. Robert E. Brodhead" cut through my prayers. I stood on trembling legs and walked to the designated spot before the Judge. For a brief moment, paranoia gripped me like a vice. What if the arrangement had fallen through? What if Parker was going to sentence me to prison after all?

Of course, I was not sentenced to prison. Parker told me that my actions were "certainly misguided," and that I had failed to set an example for LSU's young athletes, but that he believed I would never commit a crime again and that I was not "in need of incarceration or probation." He ordered me to pay the maximum $1,000 fine.

His admonishment that I had failed to set an example for the athletes at LSU cut me to the quick. I thought to myself that he would never know how right he was. Time after time, I had urged the youngsters who sat across from me in my office to stand tall and fight for what they believed in. My advice was suddenly as hollow as the sound of my guilty plea ringing in my ears.

My attorneys had arranged for a brief press conference to be held downtown near the courthouse, and I made a short statement. Thankfully, the questions were few and surprisingly kind.

Physically and emotionally beat, I found my car and headed for the LSU tennis stadium, where Kay and I had arranged to meet. The tennis team had a match that afternoon, and Kay had decided that it would easier to wait for me there than at home, alone.

Her eyes lit up when she saw me approaching. I quickly filled her in on what had transpired, and she let out a sigh of relief. It looked like our long ordeal had finally come to an end.

I took her hand, and we sat for a moment in silence, watching a tennis ball sail back and forth across the net. Then it dawned on me. Today was April 18, our wedding anniversary. For the first time in twenty-six years of marriage, I had forgotten.

CHAPTER TEN

A Kangaroo Court

Having pleaded guilty to a minor federal charge, I was anxious to put the bugging incident behind me. However, there was yet another obstacle placed in my path.

Athletic Council Chairman Billy Seay called an emergency meeting of that group for the following Monday, April 21. I learned that the council would review Judge Parker's ruling on my case and then formulate recommendations, to be presented to the Board of Supervisors on April 25, regarding my future at LSU.

Needless to say, I was infuriated by this latest turn of events. I had accepted the plea bargain because I believed that to do so would close the book on the matter. No one mentioned that the final chapter had yet to be written.

The Athletic Council had long existed for the purpose of "watchdogging" the Athletic Department. Its membership consisted of a student, alumnus and Letterman's Club representative, as well as a group of faculty and university staff members who were handpicked for service by the Chancellor. The Athletic Council had never enjoyed any real power. Until now.

I had no doubt that several council members were

looking forward to Monday's meeting. Sometime earlier, a special council subcommittee had come up with a set of policy guidelines stating its desire to have a greater role in such activities as recruiting, the awarding of athletic scholarships and the hiring of coaches. Being of the belief that *I* ran the Athletic Department, I had treated their suggestions with total disregard. In so doing, I made a number of enemies, enemies who now held my future at LSU in their hands.

I called Board member Dr. Jack Andonie, a Metairie physician, to express my fears. He told me that I was overreacting and that the Chancellor had assured the Board that the Athletic Council was being asked to review my situation for no other reason than to assure me of due process. That worried me. I had already been subjected to the Chancellor's idea of due process, and I didn't like it.

I had always enjoyed a very good relationship with the Board of Supervisors. Not once during my tenure as Athletic Director had I made a request of the Board that was turned down. Now, facing what was beginning to look like a fight for my job, I found myself one step removed from my support system.

I was informed that I would be allowed to present my case at the council meeting, and I spent the rest of the weekend rehearsing my speech. Perez and the university attorneys would be on hand to field the legal questions; all I had to do was tell the truth, the whole truth and nothing but the truth. So help me God.

I did have a number of supporters on the Athletic Council; in fact, I also had several very good friends. As I entered the building where my "hearing" was to be held, I hoped their backing would carry the day. When I saw the strained looks on their faces, however, my hope dissolved. The place had kangaroo court written all over it.

I knew the council's faculty representatives were laboring under tremendous pressures. I felt sure they had long since received their marching orders, and with fellow council member Charlie Roberts on hand to keep watch, no one would risk falling out of line.

My presentation lasted approximately an hour and a half, but after the first five minutes, it was obvious that I was wasting my breath. The flow of emotion was unilateral. Other than a few forced attempts at sympathetic smiles, my audience sat stonefaced. When I finished, no one bothered to ask me any questions. My fate, it appeared, had been sealed before I began.

What a joke, I thought to myself as I looked around the room. There was Seay, the very same person who sat in my office on several occasions and discussed what he referred to as the Chancellor's ability to manipulate the truth to his own advantage. And there was Roberts, who had kept me informed on every move the Chancellor made for three years, until he teamed up with Arnsparger and stopped calling me altogether. Who were these hypocrites to sit in judgment of me, I asked myself.

I was instructed to stand by while my presentation was considered, and I decided to wait it out at my office. As I made the drive back down the hill, I thought about the trust I placed in what Gravel had told me before I agreed to the plea bargain. I wondered if the Athletic Council members had been apprised of the reprimand, or if they were going for the kill.

As the afternoon wore on, I grew increasingly nervous. What was taking so long? I'd already been before one judge. I'd already been fined and lectured. How many times would I be tried for the same petty offense?

Word finally came that a determination had been reached, and I was asked to return to the meeting site.

The wave of emotion which swept over me during the short drive across campus took me by surprise. I thought about the trials and tribulations, the good times and the bad, and I was suddenly very sad at the prospect of leaving.

I turned my car into the crowded parking lot and walked through the group of reporters who had waited all afternoon for the council's decision. I wondered if their stories would have happy endings or if this was the end of the road for the man they'd nicknamed "Bottom Line Bob."

The air inside was thick with trouble, and the tension on the faces of my pre-meeting allies tightened my stomach. The anxiety I had felt with each passing hour was justified. I knew I was in for it when no one would look me in the eye.

Roberts cleared his throat and began to read the list of recommendations the Athletic Council would take before the Board of Supervisors on Friday:

"1. That Mr. Brodhead be issued a severe written reprimand with respect to his activities which led to his conviction of a federal offense;

"2. That he not receive salary increases or extra compensation associated with post-season or other special competition, effective immediately and for a period of three years;

"3. That he be required to comply strictly with federal, state and local laws, university and Athletic Council policy and procedure, NCAA and SEC regulations and to adhere to the highest moral and ethical standards;

"4. That the Athletic Council be instructed to review Mr. Brodhead's conduct of his duties and responsibilities of his office at the end of one year and make any further recommendations that are appropriate;

"5. That Mr. Brodhead be informed that any further action seriously prejudicial to the university shall be considered grounds for dismissal."

Only a reprimand, Bob . . .
You're overreacting, Bob . . .
Wharton is on your side, Bob . . .
Trust us, Bob . . .
Right.

I suddenly recalled a remark the Chancellor had made to me some time back regarding bowl bonuses. I had worked particularly hard to negotiate the Tigers' bids to the Orange and Liberty bowls and was more than happy to accept the customary reward. At the time, Wharton voiced his displeasure at not having received a bowl bonus himself. I had a strong feeling that I had just discovered the author of at least one of the Athletic Council's sanctions.

By the time Roberts finished his recitation, my head was pounding. I was sickened by the travesty I had just been read and was filled with resentment towards those responsible.

Of course, I should have expected as much. Seven of the Athletic Council's thirteen voting members were appointed by Wharton. On top of that, the student body representative had made it clear, through a number of public and private comments, that he was not a Brodhead backer, and the Letterman's Club delegate left no doubt that he was less than that. In fact, I had learned that prior to the council meeting, the L Club's man had made a half-hearted attempt to poll his board of directors for input on my case. When he contacted my neighbor, who served on the L Club board, he asked his wife a question, as well. "How does Brodhead act around your kids?" he wanted to know. "Wonderfully," she told him. I'm not sure if that was the answer he'd expected, or not.

I didn't ask for a tabulation of the Athletic Council's vote. I was angry, really angry, for the first time since the whole fiasco began, and I had to get out of there before seven months' worth of pent-up frustration caused me to do something stupid.

I made my way through the crowd and got into my car. I didn't know if I was more angry at the outcome of the meeting or at myself. How could I have been so trusting? Reprimand, indeed. What I had received was a public whipping.

I arrived at home in time to see that one of the local TV stations was conducting an "insta-poll." Viewers were being asked whether or not they thought the Athletic Council's recommended sanctions against me were severe enough.

The results, the anchorman proclaimed, would be aired during the 10 p.m. newscast.

I don't know why I bothered — morbid curiosity, perhaps — but I tuned in to see what the people of Baton Rouge thought of their wounded warrior. Of those who were interested enough to call in, the vast majority had voted "No." I guess they wanted my head, as well.

As the evening grew later, I began to wonder if my support on the Board would stand up to this newest assault on my character. I could envision Roberts on the telephone, calling in the Chancellor's green stamps, and suddenly, I decided that two could play that game. I got out the phone book and began placing calls of my own.

By the time I went to bed that night, I was confident I had rallied sufficient Board support to overrule the council's edict when it was presented on Friday. In fact, several Board members suggested that I make a personal appearance to present my case. I agreed. Trial No. 3 was on the docket, and this time, I wasn't going down without a fight.

The next morning, I called Doug Manship and regretfully told him that Kay and I would have to cancel our plans to join him on Wednesday for the Mexican vacation we had planned. I filled him in on the Athletic Council's proposed sanctions and my planned appearance before the Board to challenge them. He told me to go for it.

He mentioned that another couple was flying to the Baja later in the week on his company plane, and that if my plans changed, Kay and I were welcome to hitch a ride. I thanked him, but told him not to expect us. He wished me good luck, and we said goodbye.

My confidence continued to climb as Tuesday brought added support from members of the Board. Sympathetic staff and faculty members called throughout the afternoon to express their faith in me, and friends from across the state rang the Athletic Department's phones off the hook.

On Wednesday morning, I received another phone call. Unlike the calls of the day before, this one offered no words of encouragement. Instead, it summoned me to the

President's office for a meeting with Copping and Wharton. The meeting began cordially enough, as Copping expressed his sympathy with regards to my recent hardships. Then the conversation turned to the Athletic Council and its pending sanctions against me.

Apparently, my well-placed phone calls had stirred the pot, and both men admitted that I probably had enough support on the Board to overturn the council's recommendations.

When I didn't disagree, Copping asked me to consider the effect such a vote would have on the university as a whole. If the Board would indeed elect to disapprove of the Administration-backed edict of the Athletic Council, he said, the resulting rift could signal disunity. In the end, it may very well be used by anti-LSU legislators to hurt the university's appeals for state tax dollars, he said.

Perhaps my love, tarnished though it was, for the "Old War Skule" blinded me to what was being perpetrated, but I agreed to at least listen to Wharton's and Copping's plan. They said that if I would have my attorney draw up a statement in which I apologized for becoming involved in the bugging incident and then accepted the sanctions of the Athletic Council, the university would remove this blight from my record and restore any contractual items lost as a result "as soon as the heat passed." In fact, they told me, it wouldn't even be necessary for me to attend Friday's meeting, as my attorney could read the statement in my absence. Why didn't I go ahead and take that trip to the Baja I'd been planning with Manship?

Perhaps I had finally grown weary of fighting. Perhaps I was overwrought and allowing my heart to rule my head. Whatever the reason, the plan being offered by Copping and Wharton seemed so nice and simple. Just sign a statement, spend a few days on a quiet beach with my wife and my friend and leave the manipulation of the Board to the experts.

I hesitated for a moment, then agreed to their plan.

Perez and I drafted the following statement, which he would read to the Board of Supervisors on my behalf:

"Dear Chairmen:

"In the past eight days, I have stood before a federal judge and in open court, admitted my guilt, was admonished and sentenced; went before a press conference and answered any and all questions; went before the Athletic Council which also admonished me and recommended sanctions which would apply to my employment. The recommendations of the Athletic Council, in my opinion, are too severe; however, I am willing to accept the recommendation if that is the Board of Supervisors' final decision.

"I am accepting all this because I was guilty. Guilty of inventing an unimplemented plan to protect the security of my office and the future of our athletes, misguided, most assuredly, however, in the words of Judge Parker, not fatal.

"Today my case is before you, the Board of Supervisors, and as stated previously, I will accept your decision. I clearly made an error in judgment, but I hope you can understand the underlying reasons for my actions. You may rest assured that caution will guide my future actions.

"I am eager to continue my efforts to give this university an excellent Athletic Department.

Robert E. Brodhead"

This letter, which Wharton would later entitle my "admission of guilt," would ultimately end up on the list of charges he compiled against me and would have presented to the Athletic Council and, subsequently, the Board, in an effort to fire me had I not resigned first. The complete list of Wharton's charges will be detailed in a later chapter.

I telephoned Kay to tell her that I would not be attending the Board meeting, after all. I told her I'd explain every-thing when I got home, but in the meantime, start packing our bags. We were flying to Mexico Friday morning on Man-ship's plane. (This, by the way, was the same vacation the Ethics Commission would rule had violated the State Ethics Code.)

The plane stopped in McAllen, Texas, to refuel, and I headed to find a phone. Perez was standing by at a predeter-mined number in the Systems Building, and I was anxious to hear his report.

My heart sank as he told me that some of my support-ers had tried to rally for my cause, but in the end, the Board had voted to accept the Athletic Council's sanctions. I wasn't disappointed in the vote. I was disappointed in myself. I had deserted my friends on the Board who had believed in me. I had taken the easy way out.

I got back on the plane and dejectedly told Kay what had happened. I should have stayed, I told her. I should have refused to listen to Wharton and Copping. I should have gone to that meeting and fought for what I believed in.

Damn, I said to her. Damn, damn, damn.

And with that, the plane rolled down the runway and headed for Mexico.

CHAPTER ELEVEN

Mission Accomplished

To this point, I have devoted a good deal of space to disputing those things I was accused of doing during my four-and-a-half-year tenure as Athletic Director of LSU. Perhaps it is now appropriate to devote a chapter to describing those things I actually did, things which I wholeheartedly believe allowed me to leave the Athletic Department a better place than I found it.

Some of the actions I took during my administration were dictated by the seemingly impossible financial situation I inherited on June 1, 1982. Some were determined by my attempts to deter the parasitical forces trying to reattach themselves to the institutional sugartit on which they had survived for decades. The remainder of my deeds were born in and of an administrative mind trained to survive in the world of profit and loss, a world completely foreign to the multi-tiered bureaucracy of LSU.

When I accepted the Athletic Directorship I was handed two mandates by the Board of Supervisors. I was to regain financial stability as quickly as possible; and I was to achieve competitive equality with institutions of similar size and stature. I set to work on fulfilling mandate one the day I hit campus.

There are two philosophies of financial management which exist in intercollegiate sports today. The first, and more traditional method, involves entrenchment against financial pressures. When difficult circumstances arise, this philosophy dictates cutting expenses.

Philosophy number two entails meeting financial difficulties head-on with new and innovative fund-raising techniques. I am a firm believer in and practitioner of philosophy number two. The results, as you will see, speak for themselves.

The following figures detail the financial gains made by the Athletic Department during its four-plus years under my control. The figures have been compiled using university financial statements, which are available for the asking at LSU:

Year	Revenues	Expenses	Profit
1982-83	$10,534,496	$ 8,190,572	$ 2,343,924
1983-84	$11,962,217	$ 9,113,425	2,848,792
1984-85	$13,813,626	$11,940,639	1,872,987
1985-86	$15,340,932	$12,714,285	2,626,647
			$ 9,692,350

One of the most innovative revenue producers I instituted at LSU was Tigervision, the cable television network devoted exclusively to LSU athletics. Following the ESPN format of "all sports, all day," Tigervision offered taped and live broadcasts of a wide range of LSU sporting events as well as a variety of sports-related features.

When it became apparent, shortly after Tigervision was created, that television contracts between the national networks and the NCAA and/or CFA would be worth less and less in years to come, Tigervision was expanded to include pay-per-view capabilities. Pay-per-view allowed Tiger fans to purchase the cablecast of LSU football and, later, basketball games, which would be sent into their homes via a special cable system-supplied transmission box. Pay-per-view allowed thousands of LSU fans who could not purchase a ticket to sold-out football and basketball games to see the Tigers in action. At the same time, it effectively replaced the lost revenues from national network contracts.

Today, Tigervision boasts the only successful pay-per-view network in college sports, posting a profit in excess of $200,000 in 1985-86 and $400,000 in 1986-87.

The Athletic Department's concessions and merchandising programs became the most successful in the nation under the skilled guidance of Pat O'Toole. In fact, profits from concessions/merchandising at LSU compared favorably to those recorded by the University of Michigan, often referred to as the best merchandiser and concessionaire in the business. LSU's successes were particularly noteworthy given the fact that Tiger Stadium averages about 20,000 fewer fans per football game than does the 101,000-seat Michigan Stadium.

After the Athletic Department assumed control of concessions, I invested nearly $1 million in the renovation and replacement of Tiger Stadium concessions stands. Thanks to speedier service, a wider variety of concessions items and a marked increase in quality, this investment paid for itself in two years' time. Profits increased from $280,000 during 1982-83, the last year the concessions function was controlled by an outside concessionaire, to $600,000 the following year.

Just as remarkably, we were able to buy the best equipment available, no easy chore under the antiquated purchase/bid system in effect at LSU. This system, in many cases, overlooked quality for the sake of savings, but O'Toole's exacting specifications guaranteed that only the finest equipment would qualify for consideration.

To oversee the Athletic Department's ticket function, which, as I've previously explained, presented as great a challenge to fiscal control as did concessions, I hired Jim Sullivan. Sullivan, like O'Toole, is known throughout the sports world as the best in his field.

To Sullivan's absolute credit, the ticket audit performed after his first year on the job revealed a cash shortage of less than $200. In an industry which traditionally deems deficits of $20,000 as "acceptable," a $200 shortfall is nothing short of amazing.

Thanks to the promotional genius of Coach Skip Bertman, the baseball program became a pay-your-own-way sport for the first time in the history of LSU. In fact, a quick check of SEC records reveals that the 1985-86 and 1986-87 LSU baseball teams were the most financially productive in conference history.

Shortly after I arrived at LSU, I negotiated a radio contract with WJBO to become the flagship station of the LSU sports network. I was always amazed at the controversy this move created.

WWL, the 50,000-watt, clear-channel station located in New Orleans, had held the exclusive broadcast rights to LSU football games since 1942. Unfortunately, before it would carry basketball games, as well, it required a $40,000 payment per year from LSU. As a result, the Athletic Department realized a profit of slightly more than $60,000 a year for its radio rights. Having negotiated several large radio contracts during my NFL career, I immediately realized that the LSU-WWL agreement left much to be desired.

The five-year contract I negotiated with WJBO in Baton Rouge not only included football and basketball, it also generated in excess of $2.3 million for the Athletic Department.

Before I arrived at LSU, the Athletic Department suffered from an inability to publicize its sporting events in a timely manner. In fact, if the event didn't happen to be on a Saturday night and take place in Tiger Stadium, the average fan didn't know it existed.

I negotiated a contract with the local bottlers of Coca-Cola to sell Coke at all of LSU's sports facilities. In return, an electronic billboard system valued at a quarter of a million dollars was installed on campus at no cost to the university. The sophisticated signs announced all upcoming sporting events and were invaluable to the promotion of the non-revenue sports.

Above, I've listed a number of the ways in which the Athletic Department was able to make a good deal of money between 1982 and 1986. Below, allow me to enumerate several ways in which the $9.6 million in profits were spent.

The following figures were compiled, once again, using university-produced financial statements:

EQUIPMENT PURCHASES

1982-83	$ 36,000
1983-84	316,000
1984-85	366,000
1985-86	463,000
TOTAL	$1,181,000

PLANT FUND TRANSFERS

1982-83	$ 37,000
1983-84	513,267
1984-85	1,013,316
1985-86	2,761,685
TOTAL	$4,325,268

That's slightly more than $1.1 million which went toward the purchase of new equipment. Another $4.3 million were transferred to the plant fund for the maintenance, replacement and renovation of existing facilities as well as for the funding of new projects, such as the track, baseball and tennis stadium improvements. Sadly, much of the money went to correct problems which could have been avoided had there been sufficient monies to fund a basic preventive maintenance program for the university's sports facilities.

As evidenced by the $5.5 million investment in equipment and facilities repairs, the Athletic Department did not have the luxury of saving for a rainy day. In fact, had the Athletic Department not enjoyed such financial success between 1982 and 1986, LSU's sports facilities would have continued to deteriorate at an alarming rate.

Another $2 million of the Athletic Department's profits were spent in unusual and, to date, unpublicized ways. The very first $1.4 million in profit I earned went to pay off that amount of deficit which existed in the Athletic Department's fund balance. Since I had absolutely nothing to do with creating that deficit, it should have been forgiven as a debt against my administration. It was not.

In addition, during the last full year I spent at the department's helm, the university was experiencing a frightening series of budget cuts. As a result, many of its top educators were deserting the sinking ship.

To halt the mass exodus, Roberts created a giant raffle with the goal of raising $1 million for salary supplements. The fund-raiser produced only half the needed amount, however, and Roberts approached the Athletic Department for help in meeting his goal.

Given the tremendous public relations potential of such a move, I agreed. I also agreed to provide the Math Department with an additional $50,000 for equipment acquisitions. Athletics subsidizing academics would be quite a departure from the national norm, and I believed it would be looked upon favorably by the LSU community.

It may have been, had the community been made aware of it. Unfortunately, no mention was made of the Athletic Department's contribution.

Finances aside, I am most proud of the tremendous competitive strides made by the Athletic Department during my tenure.

When I arrived in Baton Rouge, the overall sports program resembled the eroded cement in Tiger Stadium. Ironically, the competitive deterioration was due, in part, to the same lack of funds which was responsible for the decay of the physical plant. Add to that a "football is king" mentality which relegated every other sport, with the possible exception of basketball, to second-class status, and it was no wonder that the LSU athletic program had sunk to the bottom of the SEC barrel.

The treatment afforded the athletes competing on the non-revenue sports teams was appalling. Not only were they served smaller steaks in the cafeteria, they waited in line behind the football team when books were issued. I put an end to both practices shortly after I arrived.

Even Academic Counseling fell into this trap, making sure the football team members were the first to receive the attention of counselors and tutors. The most sickening example of this occurred after I left, when Alisha Jones, the All-American center on the women's basketball team, was failed out of school for the lack of one quality point. According to Head Coach Sue Gunter, not one of the young lady's professors was contacted by Academic Counseling to inquire if the student might be allowed to do something to earn that one quality point.

As a part of my Five Year Plan for the Athletic Department, I set out to hire the very best coaches in every sport. I firmly believed that if a coach was not capable of winning a championship, he or she should be replaced with someone who was.

How does one assemble the best coaching talent available? Quite simply: earn enough money within the department to afford it.

I was always a little amused by the uninformed souls who turned up their noses and proclaimed that I "bought" championships. If hiring the best coaches in the country, then backing them with administrative and moral support, is buying championships, then so be it.

The group of coaches that was assembled at LSU may very well have been the best in the nation. Following are the coaches that I hired and their respective records and/or accomplishments:

Buddy Alexander, Men's Golf (1986 United States Amateur Champion; *Golf Digest* Top-Ranked Amateur, 1986; 1986

SEC Co-Coach of the Year): 12 tournament titles; 2 SEC team titles; 4 All-SEC players; 2 SEC individual champions; 4 All-Americans; 3 NCAA Top 10 team finishes.

Bill Arnsparger, Football (1984 SEC Coach of the Year, *Nashville Banner*; 1986 SEC Coach of the Year, *Nashville Banner* and *Birmingham News)*: 26 wins, 8 losses, 2 ties; 3 bowl appearances; 1 SEC championship; 3 All-Americans; 24 All-SEC players.

Karen Bahnsen, Women's Golf (1986 National Golf Coaches Association South Regional Coach of the Year; 1986 SEC Coach of the Year): 7 tournament titles; 1 NCAA tournament appearance (first in LSU Women's Golf history; 9th place finish); coached 1986 Collegiate Player of the Year, Jenny Lidback.

Skip Bertman, Baseball (1986 National Coach of the Year, *Baseball America;* 1986 National Coach of the Year, *The Sporting News;* Louisiana Sportswriters Association Coach of the Year, 1985 and 1986; 1986 South I Region Coach of the Year, American Baseball Coaches Association; 1986 Southeastern Conference Coach of the Year, *Knoxville Journal*; 1986 National Co-Coach of the Year, *Baseball America*; 1986 National Coach of the Year, *The Sporting News*; Recently named pitching coach for 1988 U.S. Olympic Baseball Team): 177 wins, 74 losses; 1 SEC championship, 1 SEC tournament championship, 2 NCAA regional championships; 2 trips to College World Series; 3 All-Americans; 5 American Baseball Coaches Association All-South Region players; 6 All-SEC players; 7 SEC All-Tournament players. There are 17 former LSU Tigers who played under Bertman who have signed professional contracts.

Phillip Campbell, Women's Tennis: 1 All-SEC player; 1 SEC singles champion; 2 SEC doubles champions.

Sam Freas, Swimming: (Men's) 18 wins, 5 losses; 2 NCAA Top 20 final season rankings (including 8th in 1987); 11 All-Americans; 7 SEC individual champions; 1 NCAA individual champion; 19 LSU individual records. (Women's) 25 wins, 3 losses; 2 NCAA Top 20 final season rankings; 5 SEC individual champions; 13 All-Americans; 23 LSU swimming and diving records.

Sue Gunter, Women's Basketball (1983 National Coach of the Year, *Basketball News*; Converse Region VI Coach of the Year, 1983): 110 wins, 37 losses; 2 NCAA tournament appearances (including Final 8 in 1986); Women's 1985 National Invitational Tournament champions; 4 All-SEC players; 1 All-American.

Scott Luster, Volleyball: 68 wins, 19 losses; 2 SEC regular-season co-championships; 1 SEC tournament championship; 3 All-SEC players; 1 All-American; 1 NCAA tournament appearance (Final 8 in 1986).

Billy Maxwell, Track: (Men's) 11 SEC individual indoor champions; 5 SEC individual outdoor champions; 5 All-Americans, outdoors; 3 All-Americans, indoors. (Women's) 11 SEC individual indoor champions; 11 SEC individual outdoor champions; 8 NCAA individual outdoor champions; 1 NCAA individual indoor champion; 13 All-Americans, indoors; 16 All-Americans, outdoors.

Jerry Simmons, Men's Tennis: 96 wins, 40 losses; 2 NCAA Top 10 final season rankings (including tie for 8th place in 1987, an LSU record); 6 individual SEC singles champions; 2 SEC doubles champions; 7 All-SEC players; 3 All-Americans; 1 SEC team title; 4 NCAA tournament appearances.

The acclaim each brought to his or her individual programs and to the Athletic Department as a whole is tribute to their talent and dedication. In four years, the Athletic Department gained national prominence, as evidenced by a survey which ranked the program second only to UCLA at the conclusion of the 1985-86 school year and third behind UCLA and the University of Texas after 1986-87.

Within the conference, LSU went from an eighth-place tie in 1981-82 to back-to-back Bernie Moore trophies in 1985-86 and 1986-87.

I resigned on December 1, 1986, with mixed emotions. I was deeply saddened by leaving the job I loved, but I was, and remain, tremendously proud of the standard of excellence the Athletic Department set under my guidance.

If I had to summarize my LSU career in two words, they would be: mission accomplished.

CHAPTER TWELVE

My
Turn

On October 7, 1986, Chancellor Wharton called Baseball Coach Skip Bertman and me to his office. He wanted to discuss the contract I had negotiated for Bertman the previous spring, the contract Wharton had approved and signed.

After a brief discussion, Wharton informed Bertman that in light of the university's current financial situation, the contract could not, in fact, be approved. He also mentioned that Bill Arnsparger had declined a pay raise because members of the LSU faculty would not be getting an increase that year. I had heard Wharton make that remark on several occasions, and it never ceased to amaze me, since I had not offered Arnsparger a raise.

By the time Wharton was finished, I was angry, and Bertman, understandably, was very upset.

As we got up to leave, Wharton asked me to stay. Assuming he wanted to discuss the matter further, I told Bertman that I'd catch up with him later.

After Bertman left, Wharton told me that he had just received word that the State Ethics Commission would be filing the charges against me I've already detailed regarding the "Bob Brodhead Show" on WJBO and the Baja trip taken at

Doug Manship's expense. He said that as a result, he had no other choice but to suspend me with pay until an internal review could be undertaken.

Suspend me! How could Wharton possibly justify such a drastic measure? The Ethics Commission's public hearing on the matter wasn't scheduled until December 18, and I had no doubt in my mind that I would beat the charges at that time. "I don't think this is fair," I told Wharton.

He didn't respond.

The next day, Wharton announced that the Athletic Council would review, as it had at the time of the bugging ordeal, my employment and make any recommendations it deemed appropriate. "If the Athletic Council's recommendation should involve changes in the terms and conditions of employment," Wharton stated, "the matter will be referred to a committee of college deans, Boyd professors and the Faculty Senate President to offer Mr. Brodhead due process. After the review process is completed, I will make whatever recommendations I feel are appropriate to the President and Board of Supervisors."

I knew I was in trouble when Wharton mentioned due process. The last time he said he was doing something towards that end was before the Athletic Council's review of my guilty plea in federal court, and we all know what happened after that.

I was so confused over being suspended that I failed to ask a few very simple questions:

Why was I being subjected to an internal review *before* the date of the public hearing on the matter?

Why was my future at LSU in jeopardy over charges which were, in the words of Ethics Commission lawyer Peter Wright, "minor"?

Why was I suspended over a radio program the Chancellor knew about and a fishing trip I had taken with his blessing?

Even Charles Cusimano, my longtime adversary, was quoted as saying, "Why are we hanging him now? That's what I want to know. They knew he was going out of the country.

We better get Charlie Roberts, too, if they're going to get Brodhead for the radio show (in reference to the fact that the Alumni Federation, under Roberts' direction, advertised on my program)."

The Athletic Council meeting was set for Wednesday, October 22. I had two weeks to formulate my defense.

I received a good deal of encouragement from friends and colleagues across the state, and several Tigers Unlimited chapters sent letters and telegrams to the Chancellor on my behalf. Their kind words deeply touched my family and me, and we were heartened by their support.

But we knew that kind words and good will weren't going to save my job. I was ready for a fight.

As the date of the meeting approached, I was given a document the Chancellor had prepared and would present to the Athletic Council in open session. The document, entitled "Athletic Council Hearing," contained page after page of charges against me, ranging from "Failure to Comply with University Policy" to "Failure to Comply with Federal Law."

I had no idea how long it had taken Wharton to compile this dissertation, but it was the farthest thing from due process I'd ever seen.

As I began to read the charges, my astonishment gave way to laughter. "Christmas cards!" I said to my attorney, Nathan Fisher. "He's including the ordering of Christmas cards as a reason to fire me?"

He sure was.

As I read the rest of the list, my confidence soared. In my opinion, there was no way these "charges" could be considered grounds for dismissal. Most of them were preposterous, and some were downright incorrect.

Suddenly, I remembered so many of the meetings I'd had with Wharton over the past four-and-a-half years. He'd call me to his office to discuss a particular issue, and after we were through, he'd hand me a memo. "I was a little rough on you in this," he'd say in regards to the memo's language, "so don't pay it too much attention." I'd return to my office and read the memo to my secretary. She'd shake her head and put it in what we called "The Chancellor's Cover-Your-Ass File."

With the council meeting just around the corner, I was chomping at the bit to dissect Wharton's charges and build my case. But each time I'd state my desires to my attorney, he'd change the subject. "We'll get to that," he'd tell me. But we never did.

Just before the date of the meeting, Fisher returned from a conference with LSU Attorney Shelby McKenzie and told me that the university wanted to offer me a monetary settlement to resign.

It's over, I thought to myself. After all I've done for the Athletic Department, I'm worth no more to them than a buyout. They want to get rid of me so badly that they're willing to put their money where their mouths are.

"Fine," I told him, my sarcasm masking my hurt, "but I don't come cheap."

On October 21, the day before the scheduled Athletic Council meeting, Fisher brought me a check for $150,000. The money, he told me, had been raised by a group of anonymous donors. I put the check in my pocket.

We drafted my resignation, which simply read:

"After consulting with my family regarding my current situation at Louisiana State University, and knowing my long-term goals, I have decided that it is in the best interest of all concerned that I tender my resignation as Athletic Director at Louisiana State University.

"Therefore, I do hereby tender my resignation effective December 1, 1986."

Four-and-a-half years after it began, the "tumultuous tenure" of Bob Brodhead came to an end.

I think my final days at LSU were best summed up by local writers Bruce MacMurdo and John Maginnis. They collaborated on a story about me, which was published a week before my suspension. I found the last paragraph particularly meaningful:

"For LSU to fire Bob Brodhead would be to turn the bottom line back on him — profitting enormously from his management genius, then dumping him when he becomes a net liability. Such a move would be fitting. Hypocritical but fitting. And Brodhead would have no one to blame but himself, for he made the mistake of viewing LSU sports for what it is instead of for what it pretends to be."

What follows are the charges which Jim Wharton had compiled against me and would have presented to the Athletic Council at its October 22, 1986, meeting. As I did with Bill Arnsparger's charges against me, I have included my response to each.

I apologize beforehand to those of you who will find Wharton's charges tedious reading. I have included them in this book because I believe they are vital to the readers' understanding of the forces I battled throughout the four-and-a-half years I spent as Athletic Director of LSU. Perhaps when you are through, you will also understand that sometimes, difficult though it may be, it's easier to throw in the towel than to answer the final bell.

"FAILURE TO COMPLY
WITH UNIVERSITY POLICY"

"A. Sale of University Rights
   1. Prior to June 1, 1985
     a. WJBO
       (1) During Fall 1982, the Athletic Department entered into a contract with WJBO for exclusive broadcasting rights to LSU athletic events. The award was made on a non-competitive basis, ignoring recommendations by the Office of Business Affairs."

On August 3, 1982, I met with Quinn M. Coco, Vice Chancellor for Business Affairs, and Graham O. Peavy, Director of Purchasing for LSU, for the purpose of discussing the proposed radio contract between LSU and WJBO.

I explained to Coco and Peavy that the $70,000 per

year the university was realizing from its previous radio negotiations paled in comparison to what it stood to gain from the WJBO deal. I found both men to be very receptive to the proposal.

On August 5, Peavy sent a memo to Coco which contained his interpretation of the state and university policies with regards to the pending radio agreement. In his memo, Peavy stated that ". . . it is my opinion there are no statutes that require the advertisement for bids."

In addition, Peavy stated that, "It is my recommendation that we publicly advertise for proposals giving consideration to such criteria as: (1) Experience, ability and expertise of the proposer; (2) the attractiveness of the network; (3) guarantee of revenue; (4) any other miscellaneous considerations. The above criteria is merely suggestion on my part, and certainly Mr. Brodhead would be encouraged to use whatever criteria he deemed practical."

In deference to Peavy's recommendation, I invited all radio stations expressing an interest in pursuing a contract with LSU to submit a proposal. I also followed Peavy's suggested criteria to a T. At the conclusion of my review, I found the WJBO proposal to be far superior to the others, and I recommended that we proceed.

In a subsequent memo from Peavy to Odrie Ortego, University Comptroller, Peavy concluded his review of the proposed contract with WJBO by stating: "Notwithstanding this proposed agreement, which with refinements appears to be an excellent agreement, I still stand by my memo to Mr. Coco, dated August 5, 1982."

Perhaps the best rebuttal I can offer to this charge has been provided, ironically, by Wharton himself. In a letter, dated August 13, 1984, to the general manager of an Opelousas radio station, Wharton offered the following explanation of the university's radio contract with WJBO:

". . . Prior to the 1983-84 academic year,
LSU marketed its own radio broadcast rights
for athletic events. The University netted

approximately $60,000 per year from these broadcast rights. The internal auditors of the University, and later the legislative auditors, reviewed the policies and procedures for handling the sale of advertising and broadcast rights. Their reports were critical of past practice. A telephone survey was made of other major athletic programs across the country . . . (and) we learned that LSU was not receiving comparable compensation, coverage or promotion; therefore, our new Athletic Director was given, as a first assignment, the task of correcting problems associated with the sale of radio broadcast rights.

"As a result, the University sold the radio broadcast rights to the Baton Rouge Broadcasting Company. During the current fiscal year, the Athletic Department expects to receive the following earnings from that contract:

"1. Direct payment $275,000
"2. Football programs
(15,000/game at
no cost to LSU) $142,000
"3. Basketball programs
(2,500/game at
no cost to LSU) .... $ 20,000
TOTAL .... $442,000 (sic)

"In addition to this compensation, the Athletic Department will obtain full coverage of men's basketball and partial coverage of baseball and women's basketball, and two five-minute programs per day to promote the total sports program . . .

"The aforementioned compensation is comparable to that received by other universities having major athletic programs, and since LSU is required to cover the operating cost of its athletic program without support from the State General Fund, this level of compensation is essential to that objective . . ."

Imagine my surprise, then, when I read that Wharton had included the WJBO contract, which he credited in the same letter with making "LSU sports programs widely available at their market value," in his list of charges to facilitate my dismissal!

> "b. Countdown Clocks
> On September 12, 1984, an agreement was reached between REB (Brodhead) and Shelly Beychok concerning the purchase of advertising space on countdown clocks with no prior approvals."

I have detailed the circumstances surrounding this charge in an earlier chapter. Here, suffice it to say that the sale of advertising rights on the countdown clocks would have fallen under the same state and university policies as did the sale of radio rights to WJBO.

> "c. MacDonald's (sic) Sign
> On April 24, 1985, Assistant Vice-Chancellor Ralph Gossard wrote Mr. Brodhead about an advertising sign in Alex Box Stadium, saying he was not aware of any contract that would provide for the display of the sign, and that in the absense of any, the sign should be removed. The sign was removed, apparently because there was no contract."

When Gossard inquired about the McDonald's sign, I told him that it was a promotional gimmick, and as such, was not covered under the specific policy he was citing. The sign was not removed; it was simply relocated to its present position behind press row.

The sign, just one of the many promotional gems created by Skip Bertman, was very popular with the fans. One inning per game, it would light up, and if the Tiger batter at the plate at the time hit a home run, everyone in attendance could redeem their ticket stub for a soft drink at a local McDonald's restaurant.

It was gimmicks such as this one that prompted a local writer to call LSU baseball "more than a game — it's family entertainment," and helped vault Alex Box attendance figures into the top five in the nation.

As a result, LSU baseball became a revenue-producing sport for the first time in the program's history.

> "2. On/after June 1, 1985
>   a. Licensing
>   On 10/5/84, JHW (Wharton) directed Mr. Brodhead, Jerry Baudin, Odrie Ortego, and Sean McGlynn to develop a policy statement that applied to the sale of rights and services of the University. Mr. Brodhead was uncooperative, according to participants, in this undertaking, only attending one meeting . . ."

I did, in fact, attend only one meeting, during which time I spent two hours listening to Vice Chancellors Ortego, McGlynn and Baudin argue amongst themselves and accuse each other of trespassing on their respective areas of responsibility.

These men were perfectly capable of setting policies for the sale of university-developed technologies. But they didn't know the lower ends of their respective spinal columns from first base when it came to the mass marketing of sports. As a result, I was so frustrated at the conclusion of our first meeting that I sent my concessions manager, Pat O'Toole, a merchandising and licensing expert, to the next meeting in my place. He returned and begged me not to send him back.

The source of our frustration was the Chancellor's attempt to equate the marketing of big-time college athletics to the sale of such things as the technology to develop soft-shell crawfish. He would have had a better shot at equating apples to oranges.

> "b. Alex Box Fence/Advertising
> (1) In a memo dated October 9, 1985, Mr. Brodhead wrote Mr. Ortego that he had reached an agreement with an individual willing to construct a fence around the baseball field in exchange for the advertising rights for one year. This was accomplished outside University policy and procedures in disregard of the Chancellor's instructions and a memo from the Chancellor dated October 5, 1984, concerning sale of revenue-producing rights. The contract is still not formalized and exists only as a verbal agreement between Mr. Brodhead and the fence constructor.
> (2) October 16, 1986, field audit questions procedures and makes note that a prior audit report (concerning a similar situation) and its recommendations were seemingly ignored.
> (3) October 9, 1985, letter to Ortego from REB explaining arrangement."

Every successful college baseball program, including those at Tulane University and the University of New Orleans, LSU's sister institution, utilizes stadium advertising as a means to produce revenues. LSU, until Skip Bertman was hired, did not.

Shortly after Bertman arrived, he and I pursued the idea of constructing an outfield fence on which advertisements could be displayed. After doing some research, we determined that the cost of such a fence, $35,000, would be more than the baseball program could afford. Therefore, we set out to find private funding for the construction project. Not only did we find such funding, but we also found people to sell the advertising.

According to our arrangement with the contractor, no money would change hands. The contractor would donate the fence to the university in exchange for the first year's advertising revenues. After the first year, all revenues generated by the sale of advertising space on the fence would belong to LSU. The amount of money we expected the fence to bring into the baseball program on an annual basis, $35,000, was more than the 1982 program had generated during the entire year.

In a memo to Wharton, Vice Chancellor of Business Affairs Odrie Ortego noted that the fence situation created "continued susceptibility of the University to embarrassment." I had no idea what he meant by that. I certainly failed to see how a financially successful baseball program would have subjected the university to anything but acclaim.

According to my review of the university policy with regards to the sale of advertising space, no bids were needed. Proposals from prospective advertisers were all that was necessary. The fence was installed with the advertisements already in place, so all that was needed the following year was a renewal check for $1,500 rather than another proposal.

     "c. Delta Airlines
        (1) On July 13, 1986, the Athletic Department entered into an agreement with Delta Airlines that apparently is outside the applicable University policy and procedure. In addition, the state bid laws may have been circumvented.
        (2) An October 17, 1986, letter from Accounting Services to Pat Cooper outlines possible

violations of agreement.
(3) A July 11, 1986, letter of agreement signed by Joe Yates on 8/13/86 documents the arrangements.
(4) The specifics of the agreement and negotiating notes are also attached."

One of the largest expenses faced by sports teams is travel. Within the LSU Athletic Department, the cost of transporting eighteen squads to locations across the country is tremendous.

I asked my assistant, Joe Yates, to utilize the expertise of a local travel consultant, and find a way to take advantage of the discounts and supersaver rates which are periodically offered by the airlines. Ted Cromwell, of Acadian Travel Agency, agreed to help, and he negotiated fixed discounts with the airlines to arrive at the lowest fares possible. Note that I said *lowest fares possible*. Doesn't that constitute compliance with state bid laws?

Delta Airlines was the successful low bidder through this process, offering a substantial savings in the cost of transporting the sports teams, as well as a thirty-seven-percent travel discount for LSU recruiters and other staff members.

A recap of the fares negotiated with Delta Airlines, as set forth in a September 29, 1986, letter from Acadian Travel Agency, follows:

Team Sport	Cost	Non-Negotiated	Savings
Baseball	$ 17,990	$ 48,930	$ 30,940
Golf	8,891	24,492	15,601
Men's Tennis	4,824	14,248	9,424
Track	86,856	250,120	163,264
Volleyball	10,982	31,756	20,774
Women's Tennis	4,918	14,630	9,712
Women's Golf	4,854	11,076	6,222

Men's			
Basketball	23,370	54,950	31,580
Women's			
Basketball	9,750	23,075	13,325
Gymnastics	8,970	23,550	14,580
TOTALS	$181,405	$496,827	$315,422

I still haven't figured out why Wharton would want to fire me for saving the university more than $300,000 a year in team travel expenses.

> "B. Personnel
> 1. Prior to June 1, 1985
> a. Credential review by Chancellor — In a memo dated 6/1/83 from JHW to REB, it was indicated that all units on campus, including the Athletic Department, must provide JHW an opportunity to review credentials before an offer is made."

During my initial interview with the Board of Supervisors on May 21, 1982, a member of the Board asked me if I wanted the power to hire and fire coaches. My response was simple: "Without it," I said, "I don't want the job."

My record of hiring coaches and administrative personnel speaks for itself. No program in the country can boast of the competitive and financial successes enjoyed by the LSU Athletic Department during my four-and-a-half-year tenure.

> "b. April 6, 1983 — Prospective Assistant Basketball Coach indicates that he had been offered job despite fact that it was being advertised at that time. Indicated also that the advertising only being done to satisfy federal regulations. At that time no prior approvals were apparent."

Why would prior approvals be needed to hire an

assistant basketball coach when Bill Arnsparger didn't need prior approval to hire eight assistant football coaches *while the jobs were being advertised?*

> "c. June 9, 1983 — The prospective Head Baseball Coach verbally made job offer to prospective Assistant Baseball Coach without required advertisement or prior approvals."

Should I waste the paper to respond to this "charge"? Naw.

> "2. On/after June 1, 1985
>
> a. October 14, 1985 — In a handwritten note to Buddy Alexander where Mr. Brodhead takes exception to Alexander scheduling a meeting with the Chancellor, there is the notation, 'Chancellor Wharton is certainly not going to determine your future at LSU. I am!'"

This item had been lined out on the copy of Wharton's charges that I had been given. Perhaps the Chancellor decided to omit this charge from his final version because it would have indicated his disregard for the established chain of command.

Alexander, the men's golf coach, was unhappy with his annual pay increase and decided to circumvent me in an attempt to remedy the situation. In so doing, he was overheard to make the comment that he didn't work for Brodhead, he worked for the Chancellor.

This remark irritated me, and I wrote the coach a nasty little note, the note referred to in the charge. Alexander, who has since become a good friend, vowed to me that he did not give the note to Wharton. I believed him. Perhaps my departmental leak had taken to providing information to The Hill as well as to the media.

"b. July 21, 1986 — Mr. Brodhead wrote what could be construed as a termination letter to Mr. Jeffers without going through proper University procedure and without proper approvals. Mr. Jeffers subsequently resigned from the University . . . Mr. Jeffers contends that he, in fact, was pressured to resign by REB and others."

Mark Jeffers first appeared on the scene as "Mike the Tiger," the mascot of LSU's Golden Band from Tigerland.

Shortly after I arrived in Baton Rouge, Jeffers came to me for help. He needed a new tiger costume, as the tail and paws of the old one were being held on with wire, and the band could not afford the expense.

He persuaded me that the mascot should come under the auspices of the Athletic Department, rather than the band, and shortly thereafter, Jeffers became something of a jack of all trades around the Athletic Department. The problem was, he more than lived up to the rest of that phrase, being the master of none.

During the summer of 1985, I asked Jeffers to contact potential advertisers for the "Bob Brodhead Show." As I've detailed earlier, Jeffers sold just three ads, and I did not ask for his help in this endeavor again. He would later state that he had "refused" to help sell ads for the program.

In January of 1986, I received a very disturbing letter from a reputable Baton Rougean and LSU alumnus detailing three highly sensitive matters which had been recounted to her by persons "who listed Mark Jeffers as their source within your department."

I was extremely concerned by this correspondence, and I asked my assistant, Joe Yates, to meet with the University Personnel Department. He did just that and was instructed to confront Jeffers regarding the information we had received. Yates was also instructed to immediately create a file on this employee. (A file is a folder into which a record of all transgressions is placed for future reference during dismissal proceedings.)

It was brought to my attention sometime after this that Jeffers had refused to order new uniforms for the basketball dance line, telling the group's choreographer that, "As soon as Brodhead's fired, there isn't going to be a basketball dance line."

Insubordination, failure to carry out instructions and disloyalty. I had finally had enough, and the University Personnel Department concurred.

> "c. July 22, 1986 — REB indicated to Chancellor Wharton that Mr. Jeffers was going to resign and therefore requested permission to hire a replacement. In effect, the case was presented to the Chancellor as a simple resignation which it was not, according to Jeffers."

During the second week of July, 1986, an official at the University of South Carolina called me to request information on Jeffers, who had applied for a position at that school. I informed Jeffers at that time that he could either resign and pursue the job for which he had applied, or he would be fired. That, in effect, made the matter a "simple resignation."

> "d. September 15, 1986 — JHW to Mr. Brodhead about the manner in which Jim Hawthorne was employed. Mr. Brodhead did not follow University policy concerning proper budget/ personnel forms or prior approvals."

Jim Hawthorne, an extremely versatile and talented radio personality, had replaced John Ferguson as the "Voice of the Tigers" in 1983 and had continued in that position until the summer of 1986. At the same time, Hawthorne had served as an advertising salesman for WJBO and handled the play-by-play radio chores for LSU football, basketball and baseball games.

When Hawthorne and WJBO came to an amicable parting of the ways, he approached me about a job in the Promotions Department.

I was happy to welcome him aboard. Who better to handle the job of promoting the Athletic Department, I reasoned, than the well-known and popular "Voice of the Tigers"?

Wharton, however, did not share my sentiments and gave me all kinds of problems in regards to this matter.

Imagine, if you will, the Chancellor of a university faced with millions of dollars in budget cuts spending untold hours arguing with me because I had appointed the "Voice of the Tigers" to a position for which he was perfectly suited.

Then imagine him including it in a list of reasons to fire me.

> "e. October, 1986 — REB not involved directly in verdict; however, the Judge in the case severely chastises REB for his apparent tactics in this personnel-related case . . ."

Allow to me digress a minute here and provide you with some background information on this charge.

Timothy Childs, a young man who lived in Houston, Texas, was a friend of then-Athletic Department photographer Ron Berard's. Childs' wife, Susan, supposedly coached an outstanding woman high school basketball player.

LSU Women's Basketball Coach Sue Gunter was extremely interested in the athlete, and when Berard told her that he knew the Childses, Gunter and I set out to learn the details of these relationships.

According to Berard, Childs and his wife were anxious to return to Louisiana. If they came, Berard told me, they would bring the athlete with them.

In addition, Berard told me that Childs was proficient

in television promotions, so I referred the matter to Tom Ficara, my Coordinator of Electronic Media.

At the conclusion of one of several meetings Ficara had with Childs, he sent me a memo stating that Childs, in fact, did not possess knowledge of television promotions, and that I should disregard any efforts to hire him to a position with Tigervision. There was some pressure brought upon the Athletic Department by Tim Childs' father, and I told the gentleman that I would look into the matter.

In the meantime, the contract between LSU and Cablevision, the entity which handled Tigervision, was being revised. The responsibility for hiring operations personnel had fallen to Cablevision, and to fulfill my promise to Childs' father, I asked the company's operations manager to interview Tim Childs. He told me that he didn't need anyone at the time, and I considered the issue closed.

Eventually, Tim Childs sued Ficara and LSU for allegedly breaking a promise of employment. The suit sought $24,000 in lost wages, $700 in moving expenses, $500,000 for loss of reputation and humiliation and $500,000 in punitive damages. I was subpoenaed to appear as a witness in the suit to be tried before District Judge Joseph Keogh.

During the trial, Berard, who was no longer employed by LSU, testified that I had summoned him to my office in March of 1983 when "news surfaced of Child's interest in returning to Baton Rouge." According to a story in the Baton Rouge *Morning Advocate*, dated August 12, 1986, "Berard said Brodhead talked to him about connections between Susan Childs (Tim Childs' wife) and the woman athlete."

On October 16, 1986 (eight days after my suspension), Keogh handed down his ruling on the case. Although I was neither named in the suit, nor held liable for any of the monetary damages, Keogh blasted me in his eight-page ruling. Among his comments:

> "Perhaps the Court is too naive, but the
> Court is shocked by the testimony in this case
> which preponderates to establish an attempt

by officials at LSU, namely Brodhead and
Ficara, to 'use' the plaintiff as an instrument to
facilitate the recruitment of the woman's basketball star, Monica Lamb, for the LSU
women's basketball team, by dangling the carrot of employment with LSU in front of the
plaintiff as an inducement to the plaintiff."

The story also said, "Keogh termed the promise of
employment as a means of recruitment of a sports star, 'a
rather callous and sordid abuse of one's position' and said
the courts, 'will never countenance such a blatant abuse of
authority.' "

I was astounded by the Judge's tirade against me,
particularly since the plaintiff had not stated in his testimony
that I had offered him a job, or that I had ever mentioned the
basketball recruit to him. It appeared to me that Keogh had
placed more credibility in Berard's testimony than he had in
mine.

Do you think it's any coincidence that Keogh and
Wharton are, according to Wharton, close friends?

Allow me to digress once again and provide you with
some information on my relationship with former Athletic
Department photographer Ron Berard.

Joe Yates was having a difficult time justifying the
amount of money being spent by the Athletic Department on
photographic equipment and supplies. He was particularly
concerned when he turned up charge slips for thousands of
dollars worth of equipment and supplies, all signed by
Berard.

At the same time, it came to our attention that many of
these items, including some very expensive cameras, were
missing. When I asked Berard about the missing items, he
told me they had been stolen.

As Yates and I launched an investigation, some of the
missing equipment reappeared. Much of it did not, however,
and the overall loss was substantial.

Shortly afterwards, a Baton Rouge narcotics squad

informed Yates that forged prescription slips for the drug
Percodan had been traced to Berard. The prescription slips
had been stolen from the office of Dr. Sonny Carona, LSU's
team dentist, and more than 2,000 tablets had been purchased.

Nevertheless, the Judge chose to call my involvement
in the Childs matter "a blatant abuse of authority."

I wonder what he would have called Dale Brown's
long-standing practice of hiring the coaches of high school
players in whom he was interested, the most recent example
of which was reviewed — and approved — by the NCAA?

"C. Budget
   1. Prior to June 1, 1985
      a. The 1983-84 budget for the Athletic Depart-
      ment was overdrafted by approximately
      $400,000 despite warnings (1/30/84).
      b. JHW, in memo on 6/21/84, reprimanded Mr.
      Brodhead for not adhering to budget policy and
      procedure."

Perhaps the Chancellor's greatest shortcoming was
his inability to grasp the economic concept of spending
money in order to make money.

The term "overdraft" implies that monies were spent
that were not available. One might overdraft the budget for
the Geology Department, for instance, but one does not overdraft the budget for a department in which profits are being
made.

Running a business within a bureaucracy was, as you
might imagine, no easy chore. Rather than attempt to explain
what the Chancellor failed to understand, I'll let the facts
speak for themselves.

The Athletic Department's financial statement for the
fiscal year ended June 30, 1984:

Revenues	$ 11,962,217
Expenses	(9,113,425)
PROFIT	$ 2,848,792

By charging me with a $400,000 overdraft, Wharton was actually, albeit unknowingly, saying that I had spent slightly over four percent more than I had budgeted. Would someone with even a simple knowledge of business economics deem that figure worthy of an attack?

Wharton failed to mention that a $2.8 million profit for the fiscal year ended June 30, 1984, represented a 300 percent improvement over the loss I inherited in 1982.

For your added reading pleasure, I've included a statement by the legislative auditor, state of Louisiana, along with his findings for the year in question.

"2. On/after June 1, 1985

    a. The 1984-85 budget for the Athletic Department was overdrafted without seeking approval again (7/11/85 handwritten response to Mr. Brodhead from JHW). JHW reprimands REB for disregarding policy and directives."

Again, the facts:

Revenues	$ 11,146,507
Expenses	(10,687,985)
PROFIT	$ 458,522

Concessions	$ 537,294
Merchandise	77,171
Tigers Unlimited	800,000
PROFIT	$ 1,872,987

The Chancellor would write me memos each year, reprimanding me for overdrafting my budget, without regard to or knowledge of how much profit the Athletic Department was making or, more importantly, how we were making it.

J. H. BURRIS
LEGISLATIVE AUDITOR

OFFICE OF
LEGISLATIVE AUDITOR
STATE OF LOUISIANA
BATON ROUGE, LOUISIANA 70804-4397

P. O. BOX 44397
TEL. 342-7237

April 8, 1985

REC'D. L.S.U. SYSTEM
APR 11 1985
VICE PRESIDENT FOR
ADMINISTRATION

Honorable Samuel B. Nunez, Jr., President
and Members of the Senate
Honorable John A. Alario, Jr., Speaker and
Members of the House of Representatives
State of Louisiana

We have examined the financial statements of the Louisiana State University and Agricultural and Mechanical College for the year ended June 30, 1984, which includes the Athletic Department on the Baton Rouge campus. This special report pertains only to the transactions of the Athletic Department on the Baton Rouge campus for the year ended June 30, 1984.

For purposes of this special report, our examination was made to test selected transactions of the Athletic Department on the Baton Rouge campus to determine the extent to which the department complied with prescribed laws and regulations of the State of Louisiana and of the Louisiana State University Board of Supervisors. The scope of examination included a review of out-of-state travel for football and basketball games and a review of the procedures used by Accounting Services on the Baton Rouge campus to process Athletic Department travel expense vouchers. Also, we reviewed the 1983 football ticket reconciliation prepared by the Louisiana State University internal auditors and performed appropriate tests of the work performed by the internal auditors.

Our tests of selected transactions of the Louisiana State University Athletic Department on the Baton Rouge campus for the year ended June 30, 1984, disclosed no conditions which, in our opinion, would justify further examination.

Respectfully submitted,

Legislative Auditor

JHB:RDH:ct

"b. In 1985-86 the Athletic Department again overdrafted the budget by $211,000 (memo of 10/9/86 from Jerry Baudin to JHW) despite warnings on 12/10/85 and 5/7/86 from Chancellor Wharton to Mr. Brodhead. During the course of this time, Mr. Brodhead was still attempting to spend more money (5/28/86 from Jerry Baudin to JHW)."

Again:

Revenues	$ 11,899,007
Expenses	(10,974,889)
PROFIT	$ 924,118

Concessions	$ 633,466
Merchandise	83,481
Tiger Vision	215,580
Tigers Unlimited	800,000
PROFIT	$ 2,656,645

I was "still attempting to spend more money" because at the time of Baudin's memo, there was a month left in the fiscal year.

The years in which Wharton accuses me of overdrafting my budgets can be summarized as follows:

	PROFIT
June 30, 1984	$2,848,792
June 30, 1985	1,872,987
June 30, 1986	2,656,645
TOTAL	$7,378,424

Need I say more?

"D. Board of Supervisors Ticket Policy
   1. Complimentary Tickets
     a. Meeting on 2/10/83 where Mr. Brodhead
     approved deviations from then-approved
     Board Policy.
     b. June 5, 1984 — Ted Stickles and Jim Sullivan
     memo to Mr. Brodhead stating that ticket policy
     did not follow Board policy and the suggested
     changes . . ."

As I've detailed earlier, I had found 4,000 seats which were somehow escaping the so-called Board of Supervisors Ticket Policy. And Wharton chose to question my "deviations" from the Ticket Policy?

I can't count the number of times the Chancellor asked me to make sure the Board members received numbers of tickets far beyond what the Ticket Policy allotted them. The President of the LSU System, Allen Copping, bought almost one hundred tickets over the number allocated to that position by the Board Policy. Wharton himself violated the policy on a weekly basis by waiting until Monday, and sometimes Tuesday after a game, to return his unused football tickets for credit — which usually screwed up the game statement which had been compiled on the night of the game!

Each time the football team was invited to play in a bowl game, violations of the Ticket Policy abounded, violations which were committed, ironically, by members of the Board.

Charles Cusimano, for instance, had a system whereby he would order a large ticket allotment, then send in separate checks from all of his "customers." That method, which assured that his name would not be connected to the transactions, was suggested by none other than James Wharton.

Several months before I was suspended, I stumbled across a most blatant deviation from the Board of Supervisors Ticket Policy, a deviation I had absolutely nothing to do with.

During the spring of 1986, I discovered that a significant number of side-court tickets for the NCAA Sub-Regional Basketball Tournament, held at the LSU Assembly Center, had been sold through that facility after I had instructed the Athletic Department's assistant ticket manager to hold them. I had wanted to make them available for sale to our jobbers and financial supporters, but when I went to get them, I was told they had been sold.

Wanting to know who was sitting in those prime seats, I asked the Athletic Department photographer to take pictures of the sections during one of the games, and to enlarge them so I might identify the people sitting there. Much to my chagrin, the photos revealed a group of people who did not qualify as jobbers or financial supporters of the basketball program.

Later that spring, when renewing the football season tickets, I reviewed my "protection list," those seats held back to be used for any last-minute, official needs. When I discovered that several of the seats which were on last year's list were missing from this year's, I assigned the task of finding them to my ingenious ticket manager, Jim Sullivan.

The Ticket Office's computer could practically talk with Sullivan at the controls, and he scoured over the ticket program until he found several of the seats in question. They were owned by a corporation called Allied Appraisal.

We called the telephone number listed by the computer, and to my amazement, it was the home phone number of the Director of the Assembly Center.

I then ran a computer printout of the man's personal ticket account and found several more prime East Side seats which had been missing. Out of curiosity, I decided to check the basketball ticket records, and I found that Allied Appraisal held several prime Assembly Center seats, as well.

In all, Allied Appraisal held thirty-two football tickets and ten basketball tickets. The Assembly Center Director held another eighteen football tickets and sixteen basketball tickets. Quite an array for a $30,000-a-year state employee.

With Allied Appraisal's apparent access to the computer system, I hesitate to think of possible deviations from the Board Ticket Policy which may have occurred and which remain undetected.

"FAILURE TO ENCOURAGE COMPLIANCE WITH NCAA RULES"

"A. Prior to June 1, 1985

In Mr. Brodhead's job description, he is held responsible for developing and maintaining procedures to insure that the rules and regulations of NCAA and SEC are met."

When I assumed control of the LSU Athletic Department on June 1, 1982, I had no way of knowing that a four-and-a-half year NCAA investigation was about to begin. And I certainly had no control over the transgressions which had been committed before I arrived.

I worked very hard to eliminate the types of practices that had caused problems in the past, and, as evidenced by the NCAA's finding at the conclusion of its lengthy investigation, I had worked very hard throughout my tenure to encourage compliance with NCAA rules.

"B. On/after June 1, 1985

1. Chinese Woman Swimmer (1985-86)

Student offered scholarship although not admissable to University because of low TOEFL score. In an attempt to meet its obligations to the student, the Athletic Department placed student in ELOP Program which is a violation of NCAA rules. University had to report to NCAA and place student on 'accounts receivable' because there was no way for her to pay back money owed for meals, housing, and ELOP expenses already incurred."

Larry Jones, in his capacity as Assistant Vice Chancellor of Academic Affairs in charge of NCAA compliance, authored this charge. Unfortunately, his version of the story is not quite correct.

Shoa Hong, the swimmer in question, fulfilled all admission requirements at LSU except scoring the required 500 on the TOEFL exam, an English proficiency test taken by foreign students. She scored 472.

When Swimming Coach Sam Freas was notified of her score, he asked me if the Athletic Department could hire her as a manager and pay her from the scholarship program. As managers and graduate assistants were often placed on the scholarship list, I agreed. I felt we had a moral obligation to the young lady, whom Freas had recruited, and she was very upset at the prospect of returning to China "shamed."

Freas told Shoa that in order for her to accept the financial aid, she would have to forfeit her final year of eligibility. She readily agreed.

She was accepted into the ELOP program, a course of study for students whose first language was not English, and agreed to become a manager for the swim team.

Before the arrangement was finalized, Freas contacted the NCAA to be sure that the situation did not violate any NCAA rules. Freas was told that it did not.

Two months later, Freas was notified that the university had placed Shoa into an "accounts receivable" category and had declared the entire matter an NCAA violation.

Apparently, the Administration had failed to contact the NCAA before rendering its own verdict in this matter.

> "2. Improperly Issuing Ticket for Recruit
> It has been reported and verified that an individual who is an athletic supporter for LSU received one or more tickets to be used for a recruit from Mr. Brodhead for the 1986 Texas A&M football game. This is a violation of NCAA rules."

During the week prior to the football game in question, a supporter called to tell me that a Mississippi high school football coach wanted to attend the LSU-Texas A&M game with two of his top recruits, and he needed tickets. Per the Athletic Department ticket policy, there were a number of tickets set aside each week to be used by recruits and high school coaches, and I called Recruiting Coordinator Sam Nader to secure three of them. He told me there were none available.

Rather than not help the coach and his recruits, I gave them three student tickets. I was later told that the coach did not attend the game. I was also later told that Nader and Bill Arnsparger notified Larry Jones of my transgression, and Jones, in turn, reported it to the Chancellor.

> "3. Improperly Provided Entertainment and Travel for Parent/Contributor
> Father of baseball player who also is a contributor to athletics traveled with the baseball team to Tallahassee. Same individual taken to dinner by Mr. Brodhead in Omaha at World Series. Athletic Department was notified and was refused permission to pay after the first occurrence as well as second."

For the past twenty years, Jay Patterson has been a loyal and valuable supporter of the LSU Athletic Department. From donating clothing to the coaches to cooking jambalaya for various support groups, Patterson is, as they say, a true Tiger.

It just so happens that Patterson is also the father of one of the finest left-handed pitchers ever to take the mound in Alex Box Stadium. Patterson was giving of his time and money, however, long before Greg could hold a glove.

In appreciation for his support, I invited Patterson to accompany the baseball team to Tallahassee to watch the Tigers play the Florida State Seminoles. He truly enjoyed himself, and I was glad for the opportunity to thank him for his loyalty to the program.

At the end of the 1986 season, the Tigers were extended their first-ever invitation to appear in the College World Series. While in Omaha, I invited several of the baseball team's biggest supporters to dinner. The group included Patterson and his wife.

Neither the Tallahassee trip nor the Omaha dinner had anything to do with the fact that Patterson's son was a member of the LSU baseball team. Apparently, the Chancellor chose to believe otherwise.

I'd like to close this section of charges against me with an incident which occurred, without my knowledge, during the course of the last year I spent as Athletic Director of LSU. I include it here because I consider it a very serious problem, as well as a possible NCAA violation. I also consider it far more worthy of investigation than the incidents which Wharton chose to look into, then include in his list of charges against me.

On September 30, 1986, Larry Jones sent Bill Arnsparger a memo with regard to a member of the football team. In order to protect the athlete, I have excerpted the memo, and where his name appeared, I have inserted the word "player."

(The "Pell checks" referred to in the memo are a form of financial aid awarded by the federal government to students who demonstrate economic need. If the recipient of a Pell Grant is a scholarship athlete, the NCAA requires that half of the amount of the check be turned over to the university which the athlete attends.)

". . . it appears," Jones wrote to Arnsparger, "that we have a serious problem with (player) in following procedures, university and NCAA.

"Last year on April 29, I placed (player) on accounts receivable with the university because he kept all of his Pell checks for '85-86, $1,800. (Player) informed me during the summer that he would pay this $900 before registration.

Since he registered for fall '86 and with no problem, I assumed he satisfied our Treasurer's Office on this account. However, I learned today that Mr. Copeland (treasurer) allowed (player) to register for fall on the condition that he would clear his present account when he received his fall '86 Pell check.

"(Player) did receive a fall '86 Pell check for $975, which he should have informed me of but didn't and which he should have turned over to Mr. Copeland but didn't.

". . . Somehow, (player) needs to settle his accounts receivable with the university which is now $1,900 and not just $900 — he had other bills, traffic tickets, etc., and the $1,900 has nothing to do with the latest $975 Pell check . . .

"Technically, (player) should be declared ineligible as he has kept three straight Pell checks and is presently $900 over for '85-86 year and $75 over for '86-87 . . ."

I am amazed that a matter as serious as this one was kept from the Athletic Director by the football coach who had compiled his own list of grievances against me and the administrator who was charged with overseeing LSU's compliance with NCAA rules and regulations.

According to university policy, a student may not register if he or she falls into the accounts receivable category. In the case of the athlete in question, the following figures represent the amount of money due and owing to the university:

Parking fines, 1985:	$ 283.00
Parking fines, 1986:	129.00
Emergency Loan, 1985:	102.00
Telephone Charges, 1985:	158.27
Telephone Charges, 1986:	381.55
TOTAL:	$1,053.82

In addition to the missing Pell Grant payments, the athlete had also bounced a check on the university, dated September 10, 1985, in the amount of $300.25.

According to NCAA policy, an athlete may not be

extended benefits which are not available to other students. Unpaid bills and missing Pell Grant checks certainly appear to qualify as a violation of this policy.

"FAILURE TO COMPLY WITH STATE LAWS"

Before I proceed with this category of charges, allow me to turn the tables a bit and present to you an incident which appeared to me to constitute a violation of the state's public records laws (RS 44:31-44:37). The incident occurred under the direction of Chancellor Wharton.

When the NCAA concluded its investigation of the LSU basketball and football programs in 1986, it compiled a preliminary list of the charges against each. Much to my surprise, the NCAA agreed to provide this list to the university a number of weeks prior to the date on which it would make its public announcement of the charges. The university's attorneys flew to NCAA headquarters in Kansas and returned with the list.

The Chancellor, in turn, handed the list over to a committee of academicians, who would conduct their own investigation into the charges. I was allowed no input into their efforts; I was, however, kept up to date on the progress they were making.

I was also instructed by Wharton that if I was questioned by the media about the activities of this select committee, I was to answer that its members were conducting an investigation by using the notes I had taken during the NCAA's interviews with LSU's athletes.

For five or six weeks, I followed the Chancellor's instructions and played cat and mouse with the media, refusing any requests for information which, in fact, the committee had in hand.

"A. Procurement
  1. Prior to June 1, 1985
    a. Tel Ra Productions Highlight Film

> (1) Contract with Tel Ra Productions for production of football highlight film during November 1982 by representative of Tel Ra and Robert Brodhead for Louisiana State University. Contract was entered into without competitive bidding, without proper University approval or required approval of Office of Contractual Review, and University officials only became aware of this matter when an invoice was presented for payment by the Athletic Department.
> (2) November 9, 1982 — letter of agreement between REB and William Orr, President of Tel Ra.
> (3) December 17, 1982 — letter of agreement for LSU to pay $3,500 for Orange Bowl game.
> (4) May 16, 1983 — letter from REB to JHW stating that he did not advertise for bids or get contract approval because 'it is purely a marketing decision.' "

Before I arrived on campus, the Athletic Department's highlight films had been produced internally. The result was a stockpile of amateurish films which I deemed unacceptable for marketing and promotional purposes.

Granted, the financial straits in which the Athletic Department usually found itself precluded the expenditure of sufficient dollars to produce quality films. But believing that you have to spend money to earn it, I set out to produce the kind of film the LSU football program deserved. Enter Tel Ra Productions.

Tel Ra had produced the great highlight films of the NFL prior to the inception of NFL Films, and I considered their work top shelf.

I had been on the job a few short months when I made this decision, which apparently gained immortality in Wharton's files. Tel Ra would not have been the low bidder on the project, but having seen what had passed for highlight films before I arrived, I wasn't taking any chances. Being ignorant of the state bid laws was, of course, no excuse.

Tel Ra filmed each of LSU's regular-season games, and when the Tigers were invited to the Orange Bowl, it didn't make sense that Tel Ra should not film that game, as well. The total cost for the 1982 highlight film was $28,000. The finished product was, in my opinion, worth every cent. The film proved to be an invaluable marketing tool, and the thirteen copies owned by the university were booked throughout the following summer.

> "b. Printing of Christmas Cards
> In January 24, 1983 memo from Quinn Coco to REB, it is noted that the Athletic Department had printed Christmas cards without going through the bid process. This occurred even after the Office of Purchasing had advised them not to do it."

What can I say? I am guilty of ordering and mailing Christmas cards to our fans and supporters.

> "c. Pre-Game Entertainment
> Athletic Department submitted check request dated 10/11/83 to Accounting Services for payment of pre-game entertainment on 9/24 in the amount of $500. A contract for this entertainment had not been executed and approved by Business Affairs. When asked for justification of the way arrangements were handled, Mr. Brodhead wrote Mr. Ortego that 'Justification is my OK. I asked Scott to take care of this on my OK.'"

You will have to forgive me. After four years, I don't remember what this charge is all about. I guess I'll have to plead guilty and throw myself on the mercy of the court.

> "d. New South Media
> At the initiation of the Athletic Director, an agreement was entered into between Robert Brodhead and New South Media, represented by John Marshall, which purportedly was to coordinate a 'replay network' of athletic events. A proper contract was never executed. There was a verbal agreement, and a letter from John Marshall to Tom Ficara of the Athletic Department which outlined terms as understood by John Marshall. This letter shows 'OK, REB,' which represents Robert Brodhead's approval. The New South Media is in court at this time. A preliminary default against Mr. Marshall was rendered on June 4, 1986. Mr. Marshall now lives in Florida."

Tom Ficara, whose television genius had spawned Tigervision, was searching for a way to produce revenues using the replays of athletic events. He talked to John Marshall from New Orleans about advertising sales and the possibility of setting up a replay network. I apparently gave my OK to a letter of understanding between Marshall and Ficara. In so doing, I added more volume to my ever-expanding file.

> "e. Charter Service
> On January 30, 1984, REB did not follow proper procedure in procuring charter service. Purchase order was not issued in advance."

I must have needed to be somewhere in a hurry.

"f. Capital City Trophies
    In March 1984, it was necessary to obtain
    administrative approval for paying invoices
    totalling $3,071.01 from Capital City Trophies.
    The trophies were received and distributed
    by the women's golf coach in exchange for
    free advertising on Tigervision programs.
    Such actions are contrary to University policy
    and the Athletic Director was warned by the
    Chancellor that any future occurrences
    would be the responsibility of that employee
    incurring the charges or the Athletic Direc-
    tor . . ."

Since we were having trouble, at that point, selling all
of the ad time available on Tigervision programs devoted to
the non-revenue sports, I decided that we could offset some
of our expenses by trading advertising time for items we
would otherwise be forced to buy.

The trophies in question were to be awarded at a
women's golf tournament, and Capital City Trophies agreed
to provide them in return for a specified amount of ad time.

Shortly afterwards, this particular phase of Tigervision was cancelled in favor of the more lucrative pay-per-view
network, and the number of Capital City Trophies ads which
had been run was not enough to fulfill our obligation. The
vendor, as was his right, asked for his money.

Wharton, rather than listen to any explanation of the
need for this type of flexibility, made a big deal of it, then
stowed it away in his hope chest.

"g. Baseball Office Facility
    On April 10, 1985, an audit report conducted
    by LSU field auditors was submitted to REB
    from JHW. The report cited numerous viola-
    tions of University procedure and possible
    state laws having to do with the Fire Code

(approved plans by Fire Marshall) and Building Codes (architectural seals). There was apparently no written contracts and/or agreements to donate said facility."

The baseball coaches' office was located in the Assembly Center, quite some distance from the baseball park. The only room in the baseball stadium itself from which the coaches could conduct business was the size of a broom closet. The situation was, at best, intolerable.

When Skip Bertman was hired in 1983, he formed The Coaches' Committee, a group of area civic leaders, businessmen and supporters whose primary goal was to help Bertman develop the finest college baseball program in the nation.

I was in attendance at the Coaches' Committee meeting when its members pledged their financial backing and professional expertise for the purpose of building an office facility to be located adjacent to Alex Box Stadium. In fact, several of the committee members, who were contractors, committed to build the structure, free of charge.

I was overwhelmed by their generosity and proclaimed once again that Tiger fans were the greatest in the world. I turned the entire project over to my assistant in charge of facilities.

Enter the petty pride of authorship so prevalent on the LSU campus. What a shame that Campus Planning chose to impede the progress of the contractors who had so graciously offered to donate the office facility to the university. How's that for gratitude?

As an aside, there were no violations of the fire code. Nor were "possible state laws" broken. By the way, what's a possible state law?

"2. On/after June 1, 1985
   a. Office Furniture
      (1) Office Furniture was delivered to Coach

Dale Brown during 1984-85. Proper bid procedures were not adhered to and that caused undue embarrassment and work for University personnel.

(2) May 20, 1985, memo from Dale Brown to Graham Peavy cites deviation from proper procedure.

(3) May 27, 1985, memo states that REB and John Drew have instructed Dale Brown on proper purchasing procedures.

(4) June 12, 1985, memo from Graham Peavy to REB, etc., stating that although proper procedures were not followed payment would be made in order not to penalize the vendor for an Athletic Department personnel mistake."

Dale Brown, true to his impulsive approach to everything, wanted new office furniture. So he ordered it.

I'm not sure how Wharton justifies charging me with Brown's impetuous deed, particularly since I did not find out about the furniture until I saw it in Brown's office.

I do apologize for the "undue embarrassment and work" the incident created for university personnel. Now, will someone please explain to me exactly how all this applies to me?

"B. State Code of Ethics"

Under this charge, Wharton details six investigations undertaken by the Ethics Commission during the time I was Athletic Director of LSU. Rather than tax your patience by including them here, I will simply refer you to Chapter Five.

"FAILURE TO COMPLY WITH FEDERAL LAW"

"1. Brodhead's letter to Board of Supervisors relating admission of guilt and assuring that caution will

guide future actions (4/25/86).
"2. Athletic Council statement with recommendation that any further transgressions would be considered grounds for dismissal.
"3. Statement by SGA General Assembly with resolution for stronger disciplinary action."

The letter to the Board referred to above is the statement Wharton and President Copping talked me into writing when they learned of my plans to upset the Athletic Council's apple cart. The letter I wrote rather than appear at the April Board meeting. The letter I wrote rather than hurt LSU's fundraising efforts in the Legislature. The letter I wrote rather than split the Board down the middle.

The letter I wrote rather than fight and cause problems for LSU.

In so doing, I fulfilled, as I had on several occasions during my four-and-a-half years at LSU, the words of Edmund Burke, who said:

"All that is necessary for evil to triumph is for good men to do nothing."

Epilogue

Closing the book on my four-and-a-half years as Athletic Director at Louisiana State University isn't easy. Watching from the sidelines after having quarterbacked the team to so many championships is painful, to say the least.

But Kay, Mindy, Amy, Jason and I will go on to better and brighter tomorrows, richer for having experienced the good times, stronger for having survived the bad.

Kay's favorite song is Paul Anka's "My Way." Somehow, those haunting lyrics are an appropriate ending to my book, as well as to my LSU career.

> *"I've loved, I've laughed and cried, I've had my fill,*
> *my share of losing.*
> *"And now, as tears subside, I find it all so amusing.*
> *"To think, I did all that, and may I say, 'Not in a shy way.'*
> *"Oh, no, oh no not me, I did it my way.*
> *"For what is a man, what has he got,*
> *"If not himself, then he has not,*
> *"To say the things he truly feels, and not the words*
> *of one who kneels.*
> *"The record shows, I took the blows, and did it*
> *my way . . ."*